rick stein's food heroes: another helping

rick stein's

BBC
BOOKS

food heroes: another helping

food photography
james murphy

location photography
craig easton

Commissioning Editor: Vivien Bowler
Project Editor: Rachel Copus
Copy Editor: Jane Middleton
Art Director: Sarah Ponder
Designer: Paul Welti
Home Economist: Debbie Major
Stylist: Antonia Gaunt
Production Controller: Kenneth McKay

This book is published to accompany the
television series entitled *Rick Stein's Food
Heroes: Another Helping*.
The series was produced for BBC Television
by Denham Productions.
Producer and Director: David Pritchard
Assistant Producer: Arezoo Farahzad
Executive Producer for the BBC:
Andy Batten-Foster

First published by BBC Books,
BBC Worldwide Limited in 2004
80 Wood Lane
London W12 0TT

© Rick Stein 2004
(www.rickstein.com)
The moral right of the author has been
asserted
Food photography © James Murphy 2004
Location photography © Craig Easton 2004
(www.driftwood-design.com)

ISBN: 0 563 48752 6

Set in Helvetica neue
Printed and bound in Great Britain by
Butler and Tanner Limited,
Frome and London
Colour separations by Radstock
Reproductions Limited, Midsomer Norton
Jacket printed by Butler and Tanner
Limited, Frome and London

contents

Good cooking is straightforward: buy the best possible produce and keep it simple. If you are going to be innovative, build on what you know. This book follows closely on from my last; it's another helping of food heroes where the quality of the raw materials is all-important. I've been less specific here in mentioning particular producers, mainly because my *Guide to the Food Heroes of Britain* is now published and contains well over a thousand producers of excellence. This is more about my favourite recipes and the food heroes who have inspired me with their cooking, but the message is the same: to cook well you must buy well.

There's a guesthouse just between Moy and Dungannon in Northern Ireland called Grange Lodge. We went there recently to film landlady Norah Brown's legendary Ulster Fry. This is the sort of breakfast that hard-working farmers dream about on cold winter days in County Tyrone, or 'great for a hangover,' as a 17-year-old on the streets of Belfast said when we stopped him for a quick comment to our camera. On the crowded plate were two types of local sausage, a slice each of white and black pudding, farm eggs, dry-cured bacon, potato-and-apple cakes, mushrooms, tomatoes and crisp-surfaced wheaten bread with a sweet doughy interior. The night before, Norah had given us the kind of Irish stew that these days you really

introduction

only dream of: carefully trimmed shoulder of lamb with what they call 'soup veg' – herb celery, parsley, carrot and leek – thickened with soft potato and pearl barley and well seasoned with salt and black pepper. Then we had an apple pie that was deep and moist, with a pastry that was not too rich and not too lean. Someone with complete understanding of the nuances of simple food cooked all this and I was left saying, with deep emotion, 'This food is just so damn nice!' Sure the company was great, the accents were thick, the craic was good, but would I have enjoyed the food as much in a three-star restaurant? It's a question we should all be asking in expensive restaurants: does this food actually fill me with boundless appreciation of how joyful life can be? I chose this reminiscence because it's at the heart of my book. Recipes that are a complete delight to eat, food that you just can't have enough of.

If I ask myself when did I last enjoy a meal that much, I would have to conclude that, in the last 20 meals eaten away from home, only a couple came anywhere near it. One was in a fish restaurant, J Sheekey, near Leicester Square in London – a half-pint of perfect pink shrimps, some oysters and a thick Dover Sole with béarnaise sauce; another was a steak-and-laverbread pie at a pub in Devon, which was

served with some of the nicest mashed swede I've eaten in a long time. Otherwise food in restaurants generally seems to lack heart, often well turned out but lacking any sense of identity, and often with too much going on on the plate. I think our palates respond better to a limited number of flavours. Another experience, this time in Southern Ireland, will help to reinforce this. During a memorable trip to film the English Market there we stayed in a rather old-fashioned but solid and comfortable hotel in Cork city – the sort of place in which my Uncle Charlie and Aunt Margaret would have felt at home. Would they, I mused, looking at the menu, have felt at ease with Grilled Fillet of Kangaroo Melba with a Peach Syrup resting on a Bed of Redcurrant Jelly served with a Glazed Brandy Hollandaise, or Tail of Crocodile, or Pave of Atlantic Shark with Foie Gras? There was a family of very respectable-looking Cork people sitting in the easy chairs next to me, reading the menu with obvious attention. 'Should we have the croc or the kanga,' they might have been saying. I'm not averse to recipes that originated abroad myself – there are quite a few in this book: Beef Rendang, Moussaka, and Osso Buco, to name a few – but it's the inharmonious confusion of ingredients in so much international cooking that irritates me.

introduction

I like to celebrate food that has character. I've already written one cookery book about it, made a couple of TV series and produced a guidebook to the food heroes of Britain and Ireland. It's all to do with identifying those generally small-scale producers of quality food – whether organic-vegetable growers, free-range-chicken farmers, artisan cheesemakers, or beer brewers – and celebrating their produce. This second cookery book does just that. A modern cookery book has to be more than just a collection of regional recipes to be worth cooking from and, while I've included plenty of those, I've also picked up ideas from the myriad ethnic cuisines that now thrive in this country. So there are Turkish Lamb Koftas, served with a great salad of shredded kohlrabi and carrot with lemon juice and toasted cumin seeds, a recipe for Sri Lankan Fish Curry that I picked up from a lady making lovely chutneys in The Lake District, a proper Pork Vindaloo from Goa and a seafood and rice dish from Valencia, *Arroz a la Banda*, which I prefer to paella, where the seafood-and-saffron-flavoured rice comes cracking hot and crusty in a shallow pan, and the seafood is served separately with aïoli. The unifying theme that runs through the book is that the recipes work best when made with the high-quality ingredients with which I'm used to cooking at my restaurants but which, thanks to farm and speciality food shops, good fishmongers, farmers' markets, mail order and the web, are now available to anyone.

I had a rather depressing conversation with the editor of a supermarket food magazine recently. She said she didn't think my guidebook would change the way most people shopped because they only pay lip service to the concept of carefully produced food where flavour counts. She said that the convenience of supermarket shopping would always win the day. People may say that they'd like to buy aged sirloin, real free-range eggs, freshly picked vegetables from farm shops or farmers' markets, or pork from pigs that roam in big fields but, generally, they'd take one of my recipes and expect to get the same results from supermarket beef.

This view was reinforced recently when I chatted to a number of butchers and meat porters at Smithfield market in the city of London. One of them said that every time he has a barbecue, people ask him why his meat tastes so special and theirs tastes so dull, 'They always buy the cheapest meat available,' he said. I asked fifteen of the butchers to taste sirloin of beef for us while filming the latest series of *Food Heroes*. We roasted three joints of sirloin, one of which was from an organic dairy farm I've only just discovered, Brown Cow Organics, Perridge Farm, near Glastonbury (perridge@zoom.co.uk). Here Clive and Judith Freake produce sweet, marbled beef with a delicate yellow fat from Guernsey steers. Next we chose a top-of-the-range sirloin from Sainsbury's, and, finally, a joint straight off the counter from the pannier market in Plymouth. The results proved that there is something behind the concept of food heroes: eleven voted for the Guernsey organic beef; three for the joint from Sainsbury's; and one for the market beef.

We've been running a series of taste tests to see whether people can tell the difference between the sort of food I'm interested in and the rest. Before this we had challenged fifteen staff at the Crown Hotel at Wetheral, on the river Eden near Carlisle, to tell the difference between free-range organic farm eggs, supermarket free range and battery eggs. Ten chose the organic farm eggs, five the supermarket free range and none chose the ones from the battery farm. Next we tested free-range chickens with fifteen members of the Godshill Women's Institute in the New Forest: eleven of them chose the free-range chicken. Results like these are very exciting. They reinforce my belief that to make these recipes really shine you need to buy the main ingredients from one of my food heroes.

1 eggs, cheese,

THERE'S SOMETHING VERY FRIENDLY ABOUT FIRST-COURSE EGG AND CHEESE DISHES. CONSIDER A COUPLE OF THEM — OEUFS EN MEURETTE AND GOATS' CHEESE AND THYME SOUFFLÉ, OR THE PUMPKIN RAVIOLI WITH SAGE BUTTER — THESE ARE THE SORTS OF DISHES I WOULD ALWAYS CHOOSE FROM A MENU. NO CONCENTRATION IS REQUIRED TO PERCEIVE THEIR DELIGHTS; THEY ARE THE SORT OF DISHES YOU SEE, CHOOSE QUICKLY, AND THEN CLOSE THE MENU THINKING, 'THAT'S JUST FINE, NOW WHAT ABOUT THE WINE?' I MAY BE BLOWING MY OWN TRUMPET, BUT I THINK ANY OF THESE THREE WOULD BE REMEMBERED LONG AFTER THE MAIN COURSE AND PUDDING WERE FORGOTTEN DREAMS.

pasta and pizza

Traditional cheesemaking in progress at
Doddington Dairy in Wooler,
Northumberland.

I have a sweet nostalgia for first courses like these 'cocottes'. They seem to come from an age when food was more innocent, and were the sort of thing that a chef from my Oxford college would produce for a lunch where the undergraduates met the Warden. It's a charming dish, best enjoyed with a pang of hunger and a glass of Alsace Riesling at about 12.30 p.m.

eggs baked in a cocotte dish with chopped mushrooms, thyme and gruyère

SERVES 6

25 g (1 oz) butter
1 small onion, finely chopped
225 g (8 oz) button mushrooms, finely chopped
The leaves from 1 sprig of thyme
Freshly grated nutmeg
6 large eggs
6 teaspoons double cream
40 g (1¹/₂ oz) Gruyère cheese, finely grated
Salt and freshly ground black pepper

1 Preheat the oven to 200°C/400°F/Gas Mark 6. Melt the butter in a medium-sized pan, add the onion and cook gently until soft but not coloured.

2 Add the mushrooms and thyme and continue to cook until all the excess liquid has evaporated and the mixture is quite dry. Season to taste with salt, pepper and nutmeg.

3 Spoon the mushroom mixture into 6 lightly buttered ramekin dishes. Break in the eggs, season them lightly, then spoon over the cream and sprinkle with the Gruyère cheese.

4 Put the ramekins into a shallow roasting tin and pour some hot water around them so that it comes about halfway up the sides. Bake for 15 minutes, until the eggs are set but the yolks are still runny and the cheese is lightly golden.

In my last book, *Food Heroes*, I mentioned that I often find myself left with lots of partly drunk bottles of red wine after the taxing job of tasting plenty of the best wine from Bordeaux, Burgundy, Beaujolais, and everywhere else in the world for that matter. I frequently make a concentrated red wine reduction by simply simmering it all with some *mirepoix* (finely diced vegetables), herbs and a little sugar. Oeufs en meurette is my favourite use for this rich, deep red wine sauce. It's one of those dishes that should be brought back on to every bistro and brasserie menu. I'm afraid there's quite a lot of work involved – the sauce, the garnish, the croûtes and poaching the eggs – but believe me, it's well worth it.

oeufs en meurette

SERVES 4

2 tablespoons white wine vinegar
4 large, very fresh eggs
A small handful of parsley leaves, finely chopped
Salt and freshly ground black pepper

1 For the sauce, melt the butter in a large, deep frying pan. Add the onion, carrot, celery and garlic and fry briskly for 5 minutes, until the vegetables start to colour. Add the stock, wine, thyme, bay leaves and sugar, bring to the boil and simmer gently for 40 minutes. Strain through a fine sieve into a clean pan, pressing the vegetables well to extract all the flavour – you should be left with about 150 ml (5 fl oz).

FOR THE SAUCE:

15 g (¹/₂ oz) butter
1 small onion, sliced
1 small carrot, sliced
1 celery stalk, thinly sliced
2 garlic cloves, sliced
250 ml (8 fl oz) *Chicken stock (see page 200)*
600 ml (1 pint) red wine, such as an
inexpensive Australian or Chilean
Cabernet Sauvignon
2–3 sprigs of thyme
2 bay leaves
2 teaspoons light muscovado sugar
1 tablespoon *Beurre manié (see page 201)*

FOR THE GARNISH:

15 g (¹/₂ oz) butter
12 button onions or small shallots, peeled
A generous pinch of sugar
85 ml (3 fl oz) *Chicken stock (see page 200)*
2 rashers of rindless dry-cured smoked
streaky bacon
75 g (3 oz) button mushrooms, quartered

FOR THE CROÛTES:

4 slices of white bread
2 tablespoons sunflower oil

2 For the garnish, melt half the butter in a small, shallow pan. Add the button onions or shallots and the sugar and cook over a medium-high heat until nicely browned all over. Add the stock, then cover and simmer gently until the onions are tender. Remove the lid, turn up the heat and cook vigorously until the liquid has reduced and the onions are covered in a shiny brown glaze. Set aside and keep warm.

3 Cut the bacon across into short, fat strips (lardons) and fry gently in the remaining butter until lightly golden. Add the mushrooms and fry until tender. Season with salt and pepper, set aside and keep warm.

4 For the croûtes, cut a 7.5 cm (3 inch) round or oval from each slice of bread and fry them in the oil for 1–2 minutes on each side, until golden. Drain briefly on kitchen paper and keep warm.

5 Bring the sauce back to a simmer and whisk in the *beurre manié*. Simmer for 2–3 minutes to cook out the flour.

6 Meanwhile, to poach the eggs, bring 5 cm (2 inches) of water to the boil in a wide, shallow pan. Add the vinegar and ½ teaspoon of salt and reduce to a very gentle simmer. Break in the eggs and leave to poach gently for 3 minutes. Lift out with a slotted spoon and leave to drain on kitchen paper. Repeat with the rest of the eggs.

7 To serve, put the croûtes on to 4 warmed plates and put the poached eggs on top. Scatter over the button onions, mushrooms and bacon and then spoon a little of the sauce over everything. Scatter with the chopped parsley and serve.

You might think that a bitter leaf like radicchio, lightly sautéed in olive oil, would not be a particularly attractive vegetable to add to the Italian version of Spanish omelette, particularly when the other drawback is that the radicchio turns black on cooking. Yet this is one of those dishes that, once tried, is always craved. I have a bit of a bee in my bonnet about our relative lack of appreciation of the quality of bitterness in food – something the Italians and Greeks in particular understand well. If you don't believe me, you must read one of my favourite cookery books, *Honey from a Weed*, by Patience Grey (Prospect Books, 2002). Try this dish, and I think you'll understand what I mean.

duck egg frittata with radicchio and berkswell cheese

SERVES 4

1 head of radicchio
4 tablespoons extra virgin olive oil
2 garlic cloves, finely chopped
6 free-range duck eggs (or 8 large free-range hen's eggs)
50 g (2 oz) Berkswell (or Parmesan) cheese, finely grated
A small handful of flat-leaf parsley leaves, coarsely chopped
Salt and freshly ground black pepper
Light green salad (see page 197), to serve

1 Trim the base of the radicchio and remove the first layer of soft, outer leaves. Cut the radicchio in half and then into thin wedges through the root, so that the leaves stay together in one piece.

2 Heat the olive oil in a 23 cm (9 inch) well-seasoned or non-stick frying pan. Add the radicchio and fry for 2 minutes on each side, until coloured and slightly caramelised. Add the garlic to the pan and cook for a further minute. Season with salt and pepper.

3 Beat the eggs with the grated cheese, parsley, ½ teaspoon of salt and some pepper. Pour the mixture over the radicchio and cook over a very low heat for 15 minutes, until golden brown underneath and almost set on top.

4 Meanwhile, preheat the grill to high. Put the pan under the grill for 1–2 minutes, until the frittata is puffed up and lightly golden. Slide it out of the pan on to a warmed serving plate. Serve warm, cut into wedges, with the green salad.

I'm such an addict of cauliflower cheese that I even remember the absurdly overcooked ones at school with affection. But making the dish properly gives me a great deal of pleasure. For a start, I use a really good cheese – mature Caerphilly, with its fresh acidity, is particularly appropriate. I also make a proper béchamel sauce, infusing the milk with the flavours of onion, bay leaf and cloves. I cook the cauliflower so that it still has a definite bite to it, and leave all the delicate, tender, pale-green leaves attached. And finally I like to sprinkle crisp, butter-fried breadcrumbs mixed with parsley over the top for a pleasing crunch.

cauliflower cheese with caerphilly and crisp parsley breadcrumbs

SERVES 4

1 large cauliflower
Salt and freshly ground black pepper

1 For the cheese sauce, stud the onion halves with the cloves and put them into a pan with the milk, bay leaf and black peppercorns. Bring to the boil, then remove from the heat and set aside for 20 minutes to infuse.

FOR THE CHEESE SAUCE:

1 small onion, peeled and halved

4 cloves

450 ml (15 fl oz) full-cream milk

1 bay leaf

$^1/_2$ teaspoon black peppercorns

30 g (1$^1/_4$ oz) butter

30 g (1$^1/_4$ oz) plain flour

175 g (6 oz) Caerphilly cheese, crumbled

3 tablespoons double cream

1 teaspoon English mustard

FOR THE CRISP PARSLEY
BREADCRUMBS:

15 g ($^1/_2$ oz) butter

25 g (1 oz) fresh white breadcrumbs

2 teaspoons chopped parsley

2 Meanwhile, for the parsley breadcrumbs, melt the butter in a frying pan, add the breadcrumbs and stir over a medium heat for 3–4 minutes, until crisp and golden. Stir in some salt and pepper, tip the crumbs on to a baking tray lined with kitchen paper and keep warm.

3 Strain the milk through a sieve and discard the flavouring ingredients. Melt the butter in a non-stick pan, add the flour and cook over a medium heat for 1 minute. Gradually beat in the milk and bring to the boil, stirring. Simmer very gently for 10 minutes, giving it a stir every now and then.

4 Meanwhile, cut the cone-shaped core from the centre of the cauliflower with a small, sharp knife, and cut the cauliflower into 5 cm (2 inch) florets. Put 2.5 cm (1 inch) of water and ½ teaspoon of salt into a pan large enough to hold the cauliflower and bring to the boil. Add the cauliflower, cover and steam for 5 minutes.

5 Remove the sauce from the heat and stir in all but a small handful of the cheese, together with the cream, mustard and some seasoning to taste. Drain the cauliflower and place in a warmed, shallow, oval serving dish, then pour over the sauce and scatter over the remaining cheese. Stir the parsley into the crisp breadcrumbs, sprinkle over the top and serve.

I have to say that the idea of buffalo mozzarella made from the milk of water buffalo reared in North Devon didn't fill me with great enthusiasm, but a trip to the lovely, remote English countryside near Holsworthy certainly did. The buffalo at Michael Greenaway's farm turned out to have come from northern Romania, because you can't buy the Italian ones. And the mozzarella was superb – soft and creamy, with that lovely, distinct farmyardy taste that is delicious in a salad.

It's amazing how often such a simple salad as this is not quite right – good tomatoes, fresh basil and buffalo mozzarella are all essential in making it a success.

tomato, basil and mozzarella salad

SERVES 4

4–8 ripe, sweet and juicy tomatoes, such as beef, slicing or vine-ripened ones

3–4 buffalo mozzarella cheeses, drained and thinly sliced

Extra virgin olive oil

A handful of basil leaves

Maldon sea salt and freshly ground black pepper

1 Slice the tomatoes thinly. Arrange the slices of tomato and mozzarella randomly over 4 large plates and drizzle with some extra virgin olive oil.

2 Sprinkle with Maldon salt and coarsely ground black pepper, scatter over the basil leaves and serve.

The origin of this dish is Chez Panisse, Alice Waters' legendary restaurant in Berkeley, California. As luck would have it, I was due to go over and meet her in September 2001 but owing to the tragedy of September 11th, it didn't happen. Hopefully one day it will, because her laid-back Californian style of cooking, with the emphasis on the best-quality local produce, has influenced me and lots of like-minded cooks. This recipe sums it all up, using St Tola goats' cheese from Inagh in Ireland, and cooked not in little soufflé dishes but in a large, oval, earthenware one, brought to the table all puffed up and brown and sprinkled with thyme. A perfect illustration of generous, hearty cooking.

goats' cheese and thyme soufflé

SERVES 4

1 small onion, peeled and halved
3 cloves
300 ml (10 fl oz) full-cream milk
300 ml (10 fl oz) double cream
1 bay leaf
$^1/_2$ teaspoon black peppercorns
75 g (3 oz) butter
40 g (1$^1/_2$ oz) plain flour
5 large eggs
The leaves from 2 large sprigs of thyme, plus a few leaves to garnish
150 g (5 oz) soft, fresh goats' cheese, such as Irish St Tola, Welsh Pant-Ysgawn or French Crottin de Chavignol, crumbled
25 g (1 oz) hard goats' cheese, such as English Village Green, or Parmesan cheese, finely grated
$^1/_4$ teaspoon cayenne pepper
Salt and freshly ground black pepper
Light green salad (see page 197), to serve

1 Stud the onion halves with the cloves and put them into a pan with the milk, cream, bay leaf and black peppercorns. Bring to the boil, then remove from the heat and set aside for 20 minutes to infuse.

2 Strain the milk and cream through a sieve and discard the flavouring ingredients. Melt the butter in a non-stick pan, add the flour and cook over a medium heat for 1 minute. Gradually beat in the milk and cream and bring to the boil, stirring. Simmer very gently over a very low heat for 10 minutes, giving it a stir every now and then. Pour into a mixing bowl and leave to cool slightly.

3 Preheat the oven to 200°C/400°F/Gas Mark 6. Separate the eggs and put the whites into a large mixing bowl. Mix the egg yolks into the sauce, then stir in half the thyme leaves, the crumbled fresh goats' cheese, the grated hard goats' cheese or Parmesan, cayenne pepper, ¾ teaspoon of salt and some black pepper. Whisk the egg whites until they form soft peaks and fold them into the mixture.

4 Lightly butter a shallow oval ovenproof dish measuring 30 x 18 cm (12 x 7 inches) and about 5 cm (2 inches) deep. Pour in the soufflé mixture, sprinkle with the remaining thyme leaves and bake for 30 minutes, until the top is puffed up and golden but the centre still soft and creamy. Garnish with a few thyme leaves and serve with the green salad.

Why Welsh rabbit? It was a joke from London about the humbleness of the ingredients required for this Welsh dish. When it became popular in England the name was elevated to rarebit. I would recommend serving it with sweet onion marmalade. A very good one is available by mail order from Rosebud Preserves (tel/fax: 01765 689174).

welsh rabbit

SERVES 4

85 ml (3 fl oz) full-cream milk, stout or dry cider
225 g (8 oz) Cheddar cheese, coarsely grated
1 slightly rounded tablespoon plain flour
1 teaspoon English mustard powder
A good shake of Worcestershire sauce
4 good shakes of Tabasco sauce
4 medium egg yolks
4 thick slices of white bread
Salt and freshly ground black pepper
Sweet onion marmalade, to serve

1 Put the milk, stout or cider and the grated cheese into a pan and stir over a gentle heat until the cheese has melted and the mixture is silky-smooth. Beat in the flour, mustard powder, Worcestershire sauce, Tabasco and some salt and pepper to taste and cook briefly over a low heat, stirring all the time, until the mixture thickens and leaves the sides of the pan. Remove the pan from the heat and leave to cool to room temperature. Then beat in the egg yolks, one at a time.

2 Preheat the grill to high. Toast the bread on one side, turn it over and spread the untoasted side with the 'rabbit' mixture. Transfer to a baking tray, slide back under the grill and cook for a minute or two, until golden brown, turning the tray around if necessary so that the mixture cooks evenly. Place the Welsh rabbit on warm plates and serve with a spoonful of onion marmalade.

Paneer is a firm Indian cheese, made by curdling hot milk with lemon juice or vinegar, then straining it through muslin and pressing into rectangular blocks. It has the unusual property of being suitable for frying, as it does not melt when cooked but stays in soft, neat little chunks. It is available from Asian grocery shops.

matar paneer

SERVES 4

275–350 g (10–12 oz) paneer cheese
3 tablespoons sunflower oil
1 small onion, finely chopped
1 garlic clove, crushed
2.5 cm (1 inch) fresh ginger, peeled and grated
2 medium-hot green chillies, seeded and chopped
1 teaspoon cumin seeds
1 teaspoon ground coriander
1/2 teaspoon ground turmeric
1/2 teaspoon cayenne pepper
2 tomatoes, skinned and roughly chopped
350 g (12 oz) fresh or frozen peas
A small bunch of coriander, roughly chopped
Salt and freshly ground black pepper
Pilau rice (see page 198), to serve

1 Cut the paneer into pieces roughly 1 x 2.5 cm (½ x 1 inch). Heat half the oil in a large shallow pan, add the paneer and fry gently until lightly golden on all sides. Transfer to a plate and set aside.

2 Add the rest of the oil to the pan, then add the onion, garlic, ginger, chillies, cumin seeds, coriander, turmeric and cayenne pepper and fry gently until the onion is soft but not browned.

3 Add the tomatoes, peas, ¾ teaspoon of salt and 2 tablespoons of water and simmer for 5 minutes. Stir in the paneer and cook gently for another 5 minutes. Stir in the coriander and sprinkle with a little black pepper. Serve with the pilau rice.

I like to make these rather satisfying pancakes with Berwick Edge cheese from Doddington. Maggie Maxwell is one of those inspiring cheesemakers who talk so passionately and knowledgeably about their artisan skill. She learnt a lot of her cheesemaking techniques from the Dutch Gouda-makers, and there is a distinct similarity between Berwick Edge and the Dutch cheese. It's very effective in a pleasant lunch dish like this.

baked cheese, ham and spinach pancakes

SERVES 6

15 g (¹/₂ oz) butter
675 g (1¹/₂ lb) spinach, washed and large stalks removed
A pinch of freshly grated nutmeg
12 small, very thin slices (about 15 g/ ¹/₂ oz each) of good-quality cooked ham
Salt and freshly ground black pepper

FOR THE SAUCE:
1 onion, peeled and halved
6 cloves
900 ml (1¹/₂ pints) full-cream milk
2 bay leaves
1 teaspoon black peppercorns
65 g (2¹/₂ oz) butter
65 g (2¹/₂ oz) plain flour
4 tablespoons double cream
175 g (6 oz) Berwick Edge, Gruyère or Emmenthal cheese, coarsely grated
1 medium egg yolk

FOR THE PANCAKES:
100 g (4 oz) plain flour, sifted
¹/₄ teaspoon salt
1 medium egg
1 medium egg yolk
300 ml (10 fl oz) full-cream milk
25 g (1 oz) butter, melted

1 For the sauce, stud the onion halves with the cloves and put into a pan with the milk, bay leaves and black peppercorns. Bring to the boil, then remove from the heat and set aside for 20 minutes to infuse.

2 For the pancakes, sift the flour and salt into a bowl and make a well in the centre. Add the egg, egg yolk and milk and beat together to make a smooth batter.

3 Heat an 18 cm (7 inch) non-stick frying pan over a medium-high heat. Brush with a little of the melted butter, pour in a little of the batter and swirl it around so that it thinly coats the base of the pan. Cook for 1 minute, until lightly golden underneath, then flip over and cook for a few seconds more. Slide on to a plate and repeat to make 12 pancakes.

4 Heat the butter in a large pan, add the spinach and cook over a high heat until it has wilted. Tip into a colander and press out all the excess liquid, then chop coarsely. Transfer to a mixing bowl and leave to cool.

5 Preheat the oven to 200°C/400°F/Gas Mark 6. Strain the milk for the sauce through a sieve, discarding the flavourings. Melt the butter in a non-stick pan, add the flour and cook over a medium heat for 1 minute. Gradually beat in the milk and bring to the boil, stirring. Simmer very gently over a low heat for 10 minutes, giving it a stir every now and then.

6 Remove the pan from the heat and stir in the cream, 100 g (4 oz) of the grated cheese, the egg yolk and some seasoning to taste. Stir about a third of the sauce into the spinach, add the nutmeg and adjust the seasoning.

7 Lay the pancakes out on a work surface and cover each one with a slice of ham. Spoon the spinach mixture across the centre of each one, roll up and divide between 6 lightly buttered individual gratin dishes. Pour the remaining sauce over the top of the pancakes and sprinkle with the remaining cheese. Bake for 25–30 minutes, until golden.

This isn't any old recipe for pizza – this is my recipe and it's worth making for the following reasons. Firstly, the dough will give you the lightest, crispest, thinnest base. The buffalo mozzarella will give you a very good-tasting cheese on a pizza, and the use of the best vine-ripened tomatoes, peeled and seeded, then concentrated in hot olive oil, will give you a really fresh tomato sauce. I add a bit of garlic and oregano too, but basically this is just a pizza Margherita, which is finished with fresh basil leaves and said to resemble the Italian flag – i.e. red tomato, white mozzarella and green basil. I'm extremely conservative about my toppings for pizzas. The only thing that I like to add occasionally is anchovy fillets, and those are the ones salted and preserved in olive oil – definitely not the ones in vinegar! These are 25 cm (10 inch) pizzas and because they are baked on preheated trays or tiles you can only cook two at a time. Obviously a pizza 'peel' is the right tool to transfer your pizza to the hot oven but you can easily use a spare baking sheet, or even a piece of cardboard or hardboard, best sprinkled with a little cornmeal or polenta to help them slide.

pizza margherita

MAKES 4 X 25 CM (10 INCH) PIZZAS

4 tablespoons olive oil, plus extra
for drizzling
2 garlic cloves, finely chopped
1^1/$_2$ kg (3^1/$_2$ lb) vine-ripened tomatoes,
skinned, seeded and roughly
chopped
1 tablespoon chopped oregano
350 g (12 oz) buffalo mozzarella cheese,
thinly sliced
A large handful of basil leaves,
torn into pieces
Maldon sea salt and freshly ground
black pepper

FOR THE BASE:

550 g (1^1/$_4$ lb) strong white flour
4 teaspoons easy-blend yeast
2 teaspoons salt
475 ml (16 fl oz) hand-hot water
4 teaspoons olive oil
4 tablespoons polenta or semolina

1 For the base, sift the flour, yeast and salt into a bowl and make a well in the centre. Add the warm water and olive oil and mix together into a soft dough. Tip the dough out on to a lightly floured surface and knead for 5 minutes or until smooth and elastic. Then return it to the bowl, cover with cling film and leave in a warm place for approximately 1 hour, or until doubled in size.

2 Meanwhile, for the topping, heat the oil and garlic in a large, shallow pan. As soon as the garlic starts to sizzle, add the tomatoes and some salt and pepper and simmer quite vigorously for 7–10 minutes, until reduced to a thickish sauce. Adjust the seasoning if necessary.

3 Put 2 large baking sheets or quarry tiles into the oven and heat it to its highest setting. Knock the air out of the dough and knead it briefly once more on a lightly floured surface. Divide into 4 pieces and keep the spare ones covered with cling film while you shape the first pizza.

4 Sprinkle a spare baking sheet or a pizza peel with some of the polenta or semolina. Roll the dough out into a disc approximately 25 cm (10 inches) in diameter, lift it on to the baking sheet and reshape it with your fingers into a round. Spread over one quarter of the tomato sauce to within about 2.5 cm (1 inch) of the edge. Sprinkle with some of the oregano and then cover with a quarter of the mozzarella cheese slices. Drizzle with a little olive oil, then open the oven door and quickly slide the pizza off the tray (give it a little shake before you open the oven door to make sure it's not stuck anywhere) on to the hot baking sheet on the top shelf. Bake for 10 minutes or until the cheese has melted and the crust is crisp and golden. Meanwhile, prepare another pizza and slide it on to the second hot baking sheet.

5 Take the first pizza out of the oven and move the second one on to the top shelf to continue cooking. Slide the cooked pizza directly on to wooden chopping boards placed in the centre of the table, scatter with the basil leaves and cut into wedges with a pizza wheel. Make sure everybody starts eating while you make and cook the other 2 pizzas.

Which Italian ever thought of combining crushed amaretti biscuits with pumpkin as a filling for ravioli? It teases me just as much as trying to figure out how someone thought that chocolate would come out of a cocoa bean or coffee from a coffee bean. But there is a memorable fusion between a good pumpkin, such as a Crown Prince or Jack-Be-Little variety and amaretti biscuits. Combine that with a simple sauce made with unsalted butter, whole sage leaves and lemon juice and you have a classic dish. Lightly sprinkle with a little extra Parmesan cheese, if you wish.

pumpkin ravioli with sage butter

SERVES 4

450 g (1 lb) piece of pumpkin
1 tablespoon olive oil
A large pinch of fennel seeds,
lightly crushed
1 medium egg yolk
25 g (1 oz) Parmesan cheese,
freshly grated, plus extra to serve
A pinch of freshly grated nutmeg
2 amaretti biscuits, crushed
15 g (1/2 oz) fresh white breadcrumbs
Salt and freshly ground black pepper

FOR THE FRESH EGG PASTA:
225 g (8 oz) plain flour
1/4 teaspoon salt
1/2 teaspoon olive oil
2 medium eggs
4 medium egg yolks

FOR THE SAGE BUTTER:
75 g (3 oz) unsalted butter
20 small sage leaves
1 tablespoon lemon juice

1 Preheat the oven to 200°C/400°F/Gas Mark 6. Cut the piece of pumpkin into wedges and scoop out the seeds. Put into a roasting tin, sprinkle over the oil, crushed fennel seeds and some seasoning and turn over once or twice. Roast for 30 minutes, until tender. Leave until cool enough to handle and then scoop the flesh away from the skin. Put into a bowl and mash to a smooth purée with a fork. Stir in the egg yolk, Parmesan cheese, nutmeg, amaretti biscuits, breadcrumbs and some seasoning to taste.

2 For the pasta dough, put all the ingredients into a food processor and blend until they come together into a ball. Tip out on to a work surface and knead for 10 minutes, until smooth and elastic. Wrap in cling film and leave to rest for 10–15 minutes.

3 Bring a large pan of well-salted water (1 teaspoon salt per 600 ml/1 pint water) to the boil. To make the ravioli, cut the pasta dough into quarters and, working with one piece at a time, roll out using a pasta machine, lightly dusting the dough with flour between rolls, and finishing on setting number 5. Place the piece of dough on a floured surface and make small indentations over the bottom half of it at 6 cm (2½ inch) intervals, 2.5 cm (1 inch) in from the edges. Place a teaspoon of the pumpkin filling on each mark and then brush lines of water between them. Fold over the top half of the dough and, working from the centre of the line outwards, press firmly around each pile of filling with your fingers to push out any trapped air and seal in the filling. Trim off the edges and then cut between the rows with a sharp knife or a fluted pasta wheel. You should make about eight to ten 5 x 5 cm (2 x 2 inch) ravioli. Repeat with the remaining pieces of dough.

4 If you are not going to eat the ravioli immediately, drop them into the boiling water as you make each batch and cook for just 1 minute, then lift out with a slotted spoon and drop into a bowl of cold water. Drain and lay out on lightly oiled trays, cover with cling film and chill until needed. Then drop back into boiling salted water just before serving and cook for 3 minutes. Alternatively, cook them all at once for a total of 4 minutes. Drain well and tip into a large, warmed serving bowl.

5 For the sage butter, melt the butter in a large frying pan until foaming, throw in the sage and fry for a few seconds. Remove the pan from the heat and add the lemon juice and some salt and pepper to taste. Pour the sage butter over the ravioli and serve immediately, with some grated Parmesan cheese if liked.

2 salads, soups

I HAD LOTS OF FUN WITH THE SALADS AND SOUPS IN THIS CHAPTER: THE HOT NEW-POTATO AND DANDELION SALAD WITH BACON AND SHALLOTS, THE SURPRISE OF YOUNG, RAW BROAD BEANS WITH A SPIKY PECORINO SALAD; THE JERUSALEM ARTICHOKE WITH A WHIMSY OF CURRY; AND THE ASTONISHING COMPLEXITY OF SOUPE AU PISTOU – THIS LAST, A PROPER VEGETARIAN DISH THAT'S FULL OF CHARACTER AND HISTORY. PEOPLE ASK ME IF I EVER GET TIRED OF WRITING RECIPES; OF COURSE I DON'T, THEY'RE ALMOST LIKE DIARY ENTRIES. I REVISIT THEM AND REMEMBER WHAT I WAS THINKING AT THE TIME, HOW I CAME UP WITH THE IDEA, EVEN A CONVERSATION ABOUT THE DISH AND THE KITCHEN WHERE I FIRST COOKED IT AND THE PEOPLE I COOKED IT FOR.

and first courses

Jekka McVicar uses organic techniques to
cultivate over 350 varieties of herbs at her farm
in Alveston, near Bristol.

One of my most enjoyable activities as a young cook was going on walks, long before my dog, Chalky, appeared, looking for wild food to cook in my kitchen. There's a great book by Roger Phillips (*Wild Food*, Pan, 1983) that I would recommend to anyone who enjoys gathering things on walks, and dandelions were a particular enthusiasm of mine. The French call them *pissenlits* – a down-to-earth description more commonly found in Anglo-Saxon English than in French, referring to the fact that they were believed to be an effective form of diuretic. Early-spring dandelions, gathered while they're still tender, have a subtle bitterness that combines most pleasingly with new potatoes and smoked bacon.

hot new-potato and dandelion salad with bacon and shallots

SERVES 4

550 g (1¼ lb) waxy new potatoes, such as Pink Fir Apple or Anya, scrubbed clean
25 g (1 oz) small, young dandelion leaves (or watercress sprigs)
3 tablespoons sunflower oil
4 tablespoons white wine vinegar
4 rashers of rindless, dry-cured smoked streaky bacon, cut into short, fat strips (lardons)
2 shallots, finely chopped
1 tablespoon chopped chives
Salt and freshly ground black pepper

1 Bring a pan of water to the boil, salted at the rate of 1 teaspoon per 600 ml (1 pint), add the potatoes and simmer until just tender. Meanwhile, wash the dandelion leaves or watercress, dry them well and put them into a large salad bowl. Whisk together the sunflower oil, 1 tablespoon of the vinegar and some salt and pepper and set aside.

2 About 5 minutes before the potatoes are cooked, heat a dry, heavy-based frying pan over a medium heat, add the bacon and fry gently until it has rendered its fat and is very crisp.

3 Drain the potatoes, slice them into a second salad bowl and stir in the dressing, chopped shallots and chives. Tip the crisped bacon and all the fat from the pan over the dandelions. Add the rest of the vinegar to the frying pan in which the bacon was cooked and leave it to bubble vigorously until reduced to 1 tablespoon. Pour it over the dandelions, toss together well, then add everything to the warm potato salad. Mix together gently and serve.

In the *Guide to the Food Heroes of Britain*, the paperback listing of well over a thousand excellent food producers, there's an entry for Allens Farm at Plaxtol, near Sevenoaks in Kent. It is one of the last remaining Kent farms to grow cobnuts and, as Samantha Petter of the farm said, 'Our ancient, gnarled trees still stand, still bearing plentiful harvests … who could fail to be moved and impressed by the sense of history, by our great-grandfathers' endeavours all those years ago? So we still continue to promote this wonderful fresh fruit against all odds, to a small, but dedicated and passionate following.'

As with so many other crops, foreign imports have decimated the local product, but every time I pick up a cluster of fresh cobnuts in the autumn I think of Kent. This salad is dedicated to those farmers who continue to produce this great favourite of mine.

young spinach-leaf salad with avocado and cobnuts

SERVES 4

100 g (4 oz) very thinly sliced smoked pancetta

450 g (1 lb) green cobnuts (you will need about 75 g/3 oz shelled nuts) or hazelnuts

75 g (3 oz) chestnut mushrooms

1 ripe avocado

175 q (6 oz) baby leaf spinach

FOR THE DRESSING:

1 tablespoon hazelnut oil

4 tablespoons olive oil

1 tablespoon cider vinegar

½ teaspoon salt

1 Preheat the grill to high. Grill the pancetta until crisp and golden, then transfer to a plate and leave to cool.

2 Shell the cobnuts and set aside. Wipe and trim the mushrooms, then slice them thinly. Halve the avocado, remove the stone, cut the flesh into quarters and peel off the skin. Cut each quarter lengthways into thin slices.

3 Whisk together the ingredients for the dressing, toss a little through the spinach leaves to coat them lightly and divide between 4 plates. Arrange the avocado, pancetta and mushrooms in amongst the leaves, scatter over the cobnuts and drizzle over the remaining dressing. Serve straight away.

This is rather more like a platter of hors d'oeuvres than a single tossed salad, but it's not quite as complicated as it might at first seem, because the same basic dressing is used with additions for almost all the individual salads. It's a paean of praise to the delights of early-summer vegetables: artichoke hearts, asparagus, celery and green beans, all dressed separately and arranged on a large platter.

salade tourangelle

SERVES 6

4 globe artichokes
Juice of 1 lemon
400 g (14 oz) asparagus tips
400 g (14 oz) fine green beans
225 g (8 oz) chestnut mushrooms, wiped clean
4 celery stalks
16 walnuts in the shell, or 100 g (4 oz) walnut halves
2 small shallots, finely chopped
A small bunch of parsley, finely chopped
1/2 teaspoon Dijon mustard
1 teaspoon chopped tarragon
2 tablespoons double cream
The leaves from 3 small sprigs of chervil
2 teaspoons lemon juice
Salt and freshly ground black pepper

FOR THE VINAIGRETTE DRESSING:
1 tablespoon white wine vinegar
3 tablespoons olive oil
1 tablespoon walnut oil

1 To prepare the artichokes, break off the stems and discard. Cut off the top half of each globe and then bend back the green leaves, letting them snap off close to the base, until you reach the hairy choke at the centre. Slice this away with a small knife, close to the heart, or scrape it away with a teaspoon. Trim away the darker green bases of the leaves so that you are left with just the paler convex-shaped heart. Drop them into a bowl of cold water mixed with the lemon juice as you prepare each one. Steam or boil for 4–5 minutes, until just tender, then leave to cool. Slice thinly and set aside.

2 Cook the asparagus and green beans separately in well-salted boiling water until just tender – about 1 minute for the asparagus and 2 minutes for the beans. Drain well, refresh under cold water, and set aside.

3 Trim the stalks of the mushrooms if necessary and then slice them thinly. Thinly slice the celery stalks. Shell the walnuts, trying to keep the halves intact. Whisk together the ingredients for the dressing and season with salt and pepper.

4 Put the artichoke hearts, asparagus, green beans, mushrooms and celery into 5 separate bowls. Add half the chopped shallots, 1½ table-spoons of the dressing and 1 tablespoon of the chopped parsley to the asparagus; the rest of the shallots, the rest of the parsley and another 1½ tablespoons of the dressing to the beans; mix the mustard into another tablespoon of the dressing and add to the artichokes with the tarragon; add the double cream, the rest of the dressing and the chervil leaves to the mushrooms; finally add the lemon juice to the celery. Season each of the salads with some salt and pepper.

5 Arrange the salads around the edge of a large serving platter and pile the walnuts in the centre.

José Graziosi, one of the sous chefs at the Seafood Restaurant, gave me this delightful recipe, which you find all over Italy. It makes use of the very early broad beans, which are so tender it's almost pointless to cook them. They are just tossed with extra virgin olive oil, summer savory, lemon juice and salt and served with a scattering of paper-thin, waxy Sardinian pecorino cheese.

broad bean and pecorino salad

SERVES 4

675 g (1¹/₂ lb) shelled baby broad beans
(ideally no larger than a child's
fingernail)
50 ml (2 fl oz) extra virgin olive oil
2 teaspoons lemon juice
¹/₂ teaspoon finely chopped summer
savory (optional)
100 g (4 oz) mature pecorino Sardo
Maldon sea salt and freshly ground
black pepper
Crusty fresh bread, to serve

1 Toss the shelled broad beans with the olive oil, lemon juice, summer savory, if using, and some salt and pepper to taste. Spoon them into a wide, shallow serving bowl.

2 Using a potato peeler, shave over thin slices of pecorino. Eat with plenty of crusty fresh bread – sourdough or ciabatta would be ideal.

Garbure is a warming ham, duck confit and vegetable soup from the Pyrenees, which has been on our menu at St Petroc's for ten years. I think the particular excitement of this soup is the saltiness of the duck confit and smoked ham hock combined with the sweetness of the cabbage that goes in at the end. Like all these hearty meat and vegetable soups and stews, it improves with being reheated the following day.

garbure béarnaise

SERVES 8–10

1 smoked ham hock, weighing
about 1.25 kg (2¹/₂ lb)
225 g (8 oz) dried haricot beans, soaked
in cold water overnight
2 carrots, peeled
2 leeks, cleaned

1 Put the ham hock into a large but snugly fitting pan and add enough cold water to cover it by about 5 cm (2 inches). Bring to the boil, skimming off any scum as it rises to the surface, then lower the heat and simmer for 1 hour. Drain the haricot beans, add them to the pan and simmer for 30 minutes.

2 celery stalks

100 g (4 oz) slice of swede, peeled

1 large onion, chopped

450 g (1 lb) large, floury potatoes, such
as Maris Piper, peeled and cut into
1 cm (¹/₂ inch) dice

6 garlic cloves, chopped

A bouquet garni of bay leaves, thyme
and parsley stalks

½ Savoy cabbage, thickly sliced

2 legs of *Duck confit* (see page 200)

Salt and freshly ground black pepper

TO SERVE:

1 small baguette, thinly sliced

1 garlic clove, peeled

A small handful of coarsely chopped
parsley, to garnish

2 Meanwhile, cut the carrots, leeks and celery lengthways into quarters and then cut across into thin slices. Cut the swede into similar-sized pieces.

3 Add the carrots, leeks, celery, swede, onion, potatoes, garlic, bouquet garni, 1 teaspoon of salt (if your hock is not very salty) and some pepper to the pan and simmer for 25 minutes.

4 Remove the bouquet garni from the pan, add the cabbage and duck confit and cook for a further 30 minutes. Then take the ham hock and duck confit out of the pan, remove the meat from the bones and discard the skin and bones. Pull the meat into small pieces with 2 forks and return to the pan.

5 To serve, lightly toast the slices of baguette and rub them with the peeled garlic clove. Put 3 slices of bread into each soup bowl, ladle over the soup and serve sprinkled with the parsley.

This is often just called soup-veg soup in Northern Ireland and is usually made using a stock made from the leftovers of a roast chicken. It's extremely popular there, so much so that you can buy ready cut-up soup-veg mix in all the supermarkets (leek, carrot, herb celery and parsley). It's an uncomplicated dish, but very enjoyable and a heartening example of good local food.

leek, carrot and herb-celery soup with pearl barley, peas and lentils

SERVES 6–8

2.25 litres (4 pints) *Roasted chicken
stock* (see page 200)

175 g (6 oz) dried 'soup mix', or a
mixture of pearl barley, red lentils
and yellow and green split peas

2 leeks (about 275 g/10 oz), sliced

2 large carrots (about 225 g/8 oz), cut
into small pieces

3 celery stalks (about 225 g/8 oz) sliced

A large handful of herb celery,
chopped (optional)

A small handful of curly-leaf parsley,
chopped

Salt and freshly ground black pepper

Fresh crusty bread, to serve

1 Put the roasted chicken stock and 'soup mix' or dried pulses into a pan. Bring to a simmer, then cover and cook for 30–35 minutes until the pulses are almost soft.

2 Add the leeks, carrots, celery, 1 teaspoon of salt and some pepper, then cover the pan again and simmer for 15 minutes or until all the vegetables are tender.

3 Add the herb celery, if using, and parsley and simmer for a minute or two longer. Serve with chunks of crusty bread.

The addition of a little curry powder gives this soup a beguiling depth; you can't really tell where the spicy flavour of the artichokes stops and the curry starts. I've also added a small amount of asafoetida, which, although it smells a bit rank in the tin, changes to an almost onion-like flavour during cooking. But the great benefit of this curious spice is that it is supposed to prevent the well-known antisocial side effect of artichokes – flatulence. With this soup, artichokes are definitely okay, and I think you'll like the shreds of spring onion, chilli and deep-fried artichoke slivers that finish it off so beautifully.

faintly curried jerusalem artichoke soup with shredded spring onions and chillies

SERVES 4

900 g (2 lb) Jerusalem artichokes
A pea-sized piece of asafoetida resin,
or $^1/_2$ teaspoon asafoetida powder
100 g (4 oz) butter
1 large onion, finely chopped
3 celery stalks, sliced
2 garlic cloves, crushed
1 teaspoon mild curry powder
1.2 litres (2 pints) *Chicken stock* (see
page 200) or vegetable stock
4 tablespoons double cream
Salt and freshly ground black pepper

FOR THE GARNISH:
Sunflower oil for shallow-frying
1 Jerusalem artichoke, peeled, halved
lengthways and thinly sliced
1 medium-hot red Dutch chilli, seeded
and thinly sliced
2 spring onions, thinly sliced on
the diagonal

1 Peel or scrub the artichokes, depending on their size, then chop into small pieces. If you are using asafoetida resin, grind it to a fine powder with a pestle and mortar.

2 Melt the butter in a pan, add the artichokes, onion, celery, garlic, curry powder and asafoetida and cook gently, without colouring, for 5 minutes or until soft. Add the stock, bring to the boil, then cover and simmer for 30–40 minutes, until the artichokes are very tender.

3 Leave the soup to cool slightly, then liquidise in batches until smooth. Press through a sieve into a clean pan and stir in the double cream. Season to taste and keep hot.

4 Just before serving, heat 1 cm (½ inch) of sunflower oil in a small saucepan. Add the sliced artichoke and fry until lightly golden. Remove with a slotted spoon and drain briefly on kitchen paper. Mix with the chilli, spring onions and a pinch of salt.

5 Bring the soup back to a gentle simmer, then ladle into warmed bowls. Sprinkle with the artichoke and chilli garnish and serve straight away.

I was listening to a programme on Radio 4 the other day, which was trying to assess the relative importance of vision over hearing in building up memory. In the end, the experts were forced to admit that it was as yet unquantifiable, as was the importance of smell, but all I can say is that the memory of my first real encounter with basil is as vivid as anything else. It was during a long, warm September in the early eighties in a friend's garden that ran down to the River Fal. The basil was nearly three feet high. Amazingly, looking back now, basil didn't feature much in my cooking before then, but it was at this same time that I came across Elizabeth David's recipe for soupe au pistou. Though my version is now slightly modified, I can still remember the intense aroma of Parmesan, garlic, basil and olive oil in the mortar and pestle and the complete exhilaration of this wonderful vegetable soup after tasting it, green with pistou.
Pistou is, of course, very closely related to the Genoese pesto, since Nice, where this soup comes from, and Genoa are so close, but unlike pesto it doesn't include pine nuts and often uses a little chopped tomato.

soupe au pistou

SERVES 6–8

100 g (4 oz) dried white beans, such as
cannellini or haricot blanc, soaked in
cold water overnight
4 tablespoons olive oil
1 garlic clove, finely chopped
A bouquet garni of bay leaves, thyme
and parsley stalks
1 onion, chopped
1 leek, cut into small dice
2 carrots, cut into small dice
675 g (1¹/₂ lb) courgettes,
cut into small dice
450 g (1 lb) vine-ripened tomatoes,
skinned, seeded and chopped
2 medium-sized potatoes, peeled and
cut into small dice
100 g (4 oz) fine green beans, topped,
tailed and cut into 3–4 pieces each
100 g (4 oz) fresh or frozen peas
75 g (3 oz) spaghettini, broken into small
pieces, or small pasta shapes
Salt and freshly ground black pepper

FOR THE PISTOU:

A good bunch (about 50 g/2 oz)
basil leaves
3 fat garlic cloves, peeled
1 vine-ripened tomato, skinned
and chopped
75 g (3 oz) Parmesan cheese,
freshly grated, plus extra to serve
150 ml (5 fl oz) olive oil

1 Drain the soaked beans. Heat 2 tablespoons of the oil in a medium-sized pan, add the garlic and the bouquet garni and cook gently for 2–3 minutes. Add the drained beans and 1.2 litres (2 pints) of water, bring to the boil, cover and leave to simmer for 30 minutes–1 hour, or until just tender. Add ½ teaspoon of salt and simmer for 5 more minutes. Set to one side.

2 Heat the rest of the oil in a large pan. Add the onions, leeks and carrots and cook gently for 5–6 minutes until soft but not browned.

3 Remove and discard the bouquet garni from the beans and add the beans and their cooking liquor to the pan of vegetables. Add the courgettes, tomatoes and potatoes, another 1.2 litres (2 pints) of water, 2 teaspoons of salt and some pepper. Bring to the boil and simmer, uncovered, for 20 minutes.

4 Add the green beans, peas and pasta to the pan and simmer for another 10 minutes or until the pasta is cooked.

5 Meanwhile, for the pistou, blend the basil, garlic, tomato and cheese together in a food processor. Then, with the machine still running, gradually add the olive oil to make a mayonnaise-like mixture. Season to taste with salt and pepper.

6 Remove the pan from the heat and stir in the pistou. Adjust the seasoning and serve in warmed bowls with some extra grated Parmesan cheese.

I thought up this very straightforward dish after a visit to a dry-cured bacon producer, Ramsay of Carluke, in Ayrshire – one of my food heroes. They pride themselves that when frying their bacon for a 'butty' it is absolutely dry – in other words, none of that white, scummy liquid comes out. As they point out, there is no need for it: the act of curing a piece of pork draws the water out of it. With cheaper bacon, it's merely put back to increase the weight, and they enjoy a good Scottish joke about paying good money for water. This is a simple bake-in-the-oven supper dish for large open-cap field mushrooms. I particularly like the garlic and parsley breadcrumbs that you sprinkle over them.

baked field mushrooms with dry-cured bacon and garlic and parsley breadcrumbs

SERVES 4

8 large, open-capped field mushrooms
15 g (¹/₂ oz) butter
6 rashers of rindless dry-cured streaky bacon, cut across into thin strips
1 small onion, finely chopped
2 small garlic cloves, finely chopped
Juice of ¹/₂ lemon
50 g (2 oz) fresh white breadcrumbs
15 g (¹/₂ oz) butter, melted
2 tablespoons chopped parsley
Salt and freshly ground black pepper

1 Preheat the oven to 200°C/400°F/Gas Mark 6. Cut off the mushroom stalks and chop them finely. Wipe the caps clean if necessary.

2 Heat the butter in a frying pan, add the mushroom stalks, bacon, onion and 1 chopped garlic clove and cook for 5 minutes, until the onion is soft and lightly browned.

3 Put the mushrooms, rounded-side down, on a lightly oiled baking tray and sprinkle with the lemon juice. Season them lightly with salt and pepper and then divide the bacon and onion mixture between them and spread it out slightly to cover them.

4 Mix the breadcrumbs with the melted butter, the remaining chopped garlic, parsley and a little seasoning and sprinkle over the top. Bake for 12 minutes, until the topping is crisp and golden and the mushrooms are tender.

I recently stayed at an *agriturismo* hotel, high up in the hills just outside Assisi in Umbria. I asked the waitress what was in the risotto for dinner that night, and she just said it was made with some very good stock; *brodo* was the word she used. And it was just that: rice, shallots, a very good broth, some Parmesan and butter, and maybe there was a sprinkling of parsley. But that was it. It was soft, with a little residual hardness left in the rice, moist, almost runny, and satisfying, with a great depth of flavour and definitely not needing anything else.

I've tried to recreate that dish by using a recipe for a *brodo* made with some slices of shin of beef. And if using ceps they should be young and firmly fresh. They are fried separately in butter, then scattered over the top of the risotto rather than mixed into it. This risotto is almost as good made with mixed wild mushrooms or even chestnut mushrooms, sometimes known as portobello mushrooms.

wild-mushroom risotto

SERVES 4

½ quantity of *Beef broth* (see page 200)
50 g (2 oz) unsalted butter
2 large shallots, finely chopped
1 garlic clove, finely chopped
250 g (9 oz) risotto rice, such as Carnaroli or Arborio
15 g (½ oz) Parmesan cheese, freshly grated, plus extra to serve (optional)
Salt and freshly ground black pepper

FOR THE MUSHROOM GARNISH:
225 g (8 oz) ceps, mixed wild, or chestnut mushrooms, wiped clean
15 g (½ oz) unsalted butter

1 Bring the beef broth to the boil and keep it hot over a low heat. Trim away half the stalks of the ceps, mixed wild or chestnut mushrooms and finely chop them. Thinly slice the remainder and set aside.

2 Melt 40 g (1½ oz) of the butter in a pan, add the chopped mushroom stalks, shallots and garlic and cook gently for 3–4 minutes, until soft but not browned. Add the rice and turn it over for a couple of minutes until all the grains are coated in the butter. Add a ladleful of the hot stock and stir over a medium heat until it has all been absorbed before adding another. Continue like this for about 20 minutes, stirring constantly, until you have added about 1 litre (1¾ pints) of the stock and the rice is tender but still a little *al dente*. The risotto should still be quite moist.

3 About 5 minutes before the risotto is ready, heat the butter for the garnish in a large frying pan, add the sliced mushrooms and some salt and pepper and fry quickly until soft and lightly browned.

4 To serve, stir the rest of the butter and the Parmesan into the risotto and season to taste with salt and pepper. Spoon on to 4 warmed plates – it should run out to cover the base of the plate in an even layer – and then spread the mushrooms out over the top. Grind over a little black pepper and serve with extra Parmesan if you wish.

This dish is designed to exalt the sweet flavour of spring peas from the Venetian island of Sant'Erasmo, which has great market gardens on it. I thought it would be a fitting dish to celebrate the abundance of peas in Norfolk in the early summer, most of which are frozen, but they can be bought fresh locally. It's somewhere between a risotto and a soup, flavoured with good stock and pancetta.

risi e bisi (rice with peas)

SERVES 4

900 g (2 lb) fresh peas in the pod
1.5 litres (2¹/₂ pints) *Chicken stock*
(see page 200)
3 tablespoons olive oil
50 g (2 oz) pancetta, diced
1 small onion, finely chopped
225 g (8 oz) risotto rice, such as
Carnaroli or Arborio
15 g (¹/₂ oz) butter
A small handful of parsley leaves,
chopped
25 g (1 oz) Parmesan cheese,
freshly grated
Salt and freshly ground black pepper

1 Shell the peas, reserving the pods. You should be left with about 175 g (6 oz) shelled peas. Put the stock into a pan with the pea pods, bring to the boil and leave to simmer for 20 minutes. Strain into a clean pan, pressing out all the liquid with the back of a wooden spoon, and keep hot.

2 Heat the olive oil in a medium-sized pan, add the pancetta and onion and fry gently until the onion is soft but not browned. Add the stock and the rice, bring to the boil and simmer very gently for about 15 minutes, stirring once or twice.

3 Stir in the peas and cook for a further 5 minutes or until the peas are tender. Finally stir in the butter, parsley and Parmesan and season to taste with salt and pepper. Ladle into warmed soup bowls and eat as you would soup, with a spoon rather than a fork.

This is an Alsace version of a quiche Lorraine and, like that famous tart, it benefits from being made with very few ingredients – namely bacon, onions, cream, eggs and pastry. As I was moved to consider on the television programme accompanying this book, the standard long-cooked, cold quiche with soggy pastry, served at numerous unsatisfactory cold buffets, is a million miles away from a tart like this, with its lightly set, creamy filling and lovely crumbly short pastry, served straight from the oven.

bacon and onion tart from the alsace

SERVES 8

1 quantity of *Rich shortcrust pastry*
(see page 201)
40 g (1¹/₂ oz) butter or goose fat
450 g (1 lb) onions, thinly sliced
3 large eggs, beaten
100 g (4 oz) rindless dry-cured back
bacon, cut across into thin strips
300 ml (10 fl oz) double cream
10 gratings of fresh nutmeg
Salt and freshly ground black pepper

1 Roll out the pastry thinly on a lightly floured surface and use to line a loose-bottomed 25 cm (10 inch) flan tin, 4 cm (1½ inches) deep. Prick the base here and there with a fork and chill for 20 minutes.

2 Meanwhile, melt 25 g (1 oz) of the butter or goose fat in a large frying pan, add the onions and some salt and pepper and cook over a low heat for 20–30 minutes, until very soft but not browned.

3 Preheat the oven to 200°C/400°F/Gas Mark 6. Line the pastry case with greaseproof paper, cover the base with a thin layer of baking beans and bake for 15 minutes. Remove the paper and beans and return the pastry case to the oven for 3–4 minutes. Remove, brush the inside of the case with a little of the beaten egg and return to the oven once more for 2 minutes. Remove from the oven and lower the temperature to 190°C/375°F/Gas Mark 5.

4 Spread the onions over the base of the pastry case. Melt the rest of the butter or goose fat in the frying pan, add the bacon and fry until lightly golden. Scatter over the top of the onions.

5 Mix the eggs with the cream, nutmeg, some salt and black pepper. Pour over the onions and bake the tart for 25–30 minutes, until just set and lightly browned on top. Remove from the oven and leave to cool slightly before serving.

3

fish and

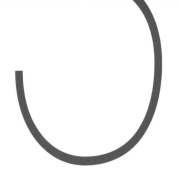

THE MOST LYRICAL FISHING I HAVE EXPERIENCED
DURING THE FILMING OF *FOOD HEROES* TOOK
PLACE RECENTLY ON A FAINT NOVEMBER AFTER-
NOON AT CLOVELLY IN DEVON, WHERE THEY HAVE A
LATE RUN OF SMALL, SWEET HERRING IN THE BAY.
WE CAST A SMALL NET INTO THE LIMPID SEA AND I
STRUCK UP A CONVERSATION WITH THE SKIPPER OF
THE TINY TWO-MASTED PICAROONER ABOUT
CONNECTIONS BETWEEN CLOVELLY AND PADSTOW.
WE HAULED IN AN AMPLE CATCH OF SILVER
DARLINGS, THEIR BACKS FLASHING WITH BLUE AND
GREEN, AND GAZED AT THE SOFT CLOUDS AS THE
EVENING APPROACHED.

I TOOK SOME OF THE FISH HOME TO MY SON
EDWARD'S HOUSE WHERE I DUSTED THEM WITH
WHOLEMEAL FLOUR AND FRIED THEM IN OLIVE OIL.
I SWEAR I HAVE NEVER EATEN MORE RAVENOUSLY.

shellfish

Coracle fishing at Carmarthen, South Wales. An ancient fishing technique dating back to Neolithic times, coracle fishing is now principally confined to

This is my interpretation of the dish that you find everywhere in France as *saumon mariné a l'anèthe*. It's quite like gravlax but the salmon is more raw. I probably enjoy salmon raw or lightly 'cooked' in citrus juice more than any other way. The aniseed taste of the Pernod complements the flavour of the dill beautifully. You could also use anisette, a slightly sweet aniseed-flavoured liqueur, but if using, just leave out the sugar.

salmon marinated with dill and pernod

SERVES 4

400 g (14 oz) piece of unskinned
salmon fillet
85 ml (3 fl oz) sunflower oil
Juice of $1/2$ lemon
1 tablespoon chopped dill
2 teaspoons Pernod
1 teaspoon caster sugar
1 teaspoon chopped chives
$1/2$ teaspoon of salt and 10 turns of the
black pepper mill

1 Put 4 plates into the fridge together with the salmon fillet and leave them to get really cold. Shortly before serving, mix all the remaining ingredients together in a bowl.

2 Put the salmon fillet skin-side down on a board. Hold a long, thin-bladed knife at a 45-degree angle and, starting at the tail end of the fillet, cut the salmon into very thin slices. Lay the slices, slightly overlapping, on each chilled plate and spoon over the dressing. Leave for 5 minutes before serving.

I have a rather single-minded enthusiasm for bass with fennel. One of my favourite recipes is to grill a whole small bass on a barbecue with fennel herb in the cavity and also between the fish and a fish wire and serve it with a mayonnaise containing lots of fennel herb and a little Pernod. This recipe is just as good but the flavour is soft, delicate and elusive. I use poached fennel and fennel herb to finish the dish but also a few fennel seeds in the stock.

There's really only one wine I like drinking with this dish – white Cassis. And I'm writing this as the temperature has just touched 37°C and I'm not where I should be – which is by a beach somewhere, eating lunch.

grilled sea bass in a clear seafood consommé with poached fennel

SERVES 4

3 bulbs of fennel
4 x 175–200 g (6–7 oz) unskinned fillets of sea bass, scales removed
A little sunflower oil, for brushing
Salt and freshly ground black pepper
A few sprigs of fennel, fennel herb or fennel tops, to garnish

FOR THE CONSOMMÉ:
1/2 small onion, roughly chopped
1/2 leek, roughly chopped
1/2 carrot, roughly chopped
1 celery stalk, roughly chopped
100 g (4 oz) unpeeled North Atlantic prawns
1 teaspoon tomato purée
1 medium-hot red chilli, chopped
1 cm (1/2 inch) piece of fresh ginger, chopped
1/2 star anise
A small pinch of fennel seeds, lightly crushed
100 g (4 oz) skinned whiting fillet, roughly chopped
1.75 litres (3 pints) *Chicken stock* (see page 200)
1 1/2 tablespoons Thai fish sauce (*nam pla*)
2 egg whites

1 For the consommé, put the onion, leek, carrot, celery, the unpeeled prawns, tomato purée, chilli, ginger, star anise, fennel seeds and whiting fillet into a food processor and blend to a fine paste, using the pulse button.

2 Put the cold chicken stock, Thai fish sauce and egg whites into a large pan and whisk together briefly, then add the contents of the food processor. Place over a medium heat and bring slowly to the boil, giving the mixture a stir every now and then. As soon as it comes to the boil, allow it to boil vigorously for 5–10 seconds, then lower the heat and leave to simmer undisturbed for 30 minutes. Pass the consommé into a clean pan through a fine sieve lined with a double thickness of muslin.

3 Remove the outer layer of each bulb of fennel and then cut the bulb down through the root into thin slices – you need about 12 slices in total.

4 Preheat the grill to high. Season the consommé with about 1/2 teaspoon of salt, bring back to the boil and add the fennel slices. Simmer for 4–5 minutes, until tender, then turn off the heat.

5 Brush the sea bass fillets lightly on both sides with some oil and season with salt and pepper. Place skin-side up on an oiled baking tray and grill for 4–5 minutes, until cooked through.

6 To serve, divide the poached fennel slices between 4 warmed, deep bistro-style bowls and place the fish on top. Pour the seafood consommé into the bowls and garnish with the fennel or coriander sprigs.

This recipe came about as a result of an evening spent at the Portuguese club in St Helier on the island of Jersey. The Portuguese serve these sardines on thick slices of bread. It's the perfect *al fresco* dish as, to eat it, you lift the fillets off the bones, eat the fillets and throw away the bones, then eat the bread, which by now is soaked with oil, adding some salad, if you like.

portuguese barbecued sardines with piri-piri oil

SERVES 4

12–16 fresh sardines
Crusty bread, thickly sliced, to serve

FOR THE PIRI-PIRI OIL:
1 garlic clove, finely chopped
Finely grated zest and the juice of
1 small lemon
¹/₂ teaspoon crushed, dried chilli flakes
120 ml (4 fl oz) olive oil

FOR THE SALAD:
4–6 large, vine-ripened tomatoes,
thinly sliced
1 red onion, thinly sliced
2 small *Roasted red peppers* (see page
201), thinly sliced
Salt and freshly ground black pepper.
50 g (2 oz) well-flavoured black olives
Extra virgin olive oil and red wine
vinegar, to serve

1 To prepare the sardines, rub off the scales with your thumb, working under running cold water, then gut them and trim off the fins.

2 To make the piri-piri oil, simply mix all the ingredients together and season with a little salt and pepper.

3 If you are using a charcoal barbecue, light it 30–40 minutes before you want to start cooking. If using a gas barbecue, light it 10 minutes beforehand.

4 Meanwhile, for the salad, arrange the sliced tomatoes over a large serving plate and sprinkle with the sliced onion and roasted peppers. Season with salt and pepper, scatter over the olives and drizzle with a little oil and vinegar.

5 When you are ready to cook, the charcoal should be covered in a layer of white ash. Make 3 shallow slashes on either side of each fish and then brush generously inside and out with the piri-piri oil. Cook them on the barbecue for 3 minutes on each side, until the skin blisters and chars a little bit and the eyes turn opaque. Serve them on the slices of bread with some of the salad to follow.

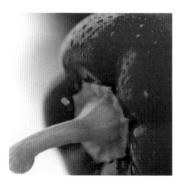

I picked this recipe idea up from a magazine I read called *The Week*. It's rather good; a potted digest of all the week's news with a pick of food journalists' recipes and restaurant reviews, too.
This refreshing recipe works equally well with all types of oily fish, such as herring, mackerel and salmon.

japanese fishcakes with ginger and spring onions

SERVES 4

3 rainbow trout, filleted (you need about 500 g/1¼ lb fillets in total)
4 cm (1½ inch) piece of fresh ginger, peeled and very finely chopped
3 fat spring onions, finely chopped
4 chestnut mushrooms, finely chopped
A little oil, for frying
Salt and freshly ground black pepper

FOR THE SALAD:
100 g (4 oz) rocket
2 teaspoons dark soy sauce
1 teaspoon roasted sesame oil
1 teaspoon cold water
Pinch of caster sugar

1 Skin and then pin-bone the trout fillets and then cut them lengthways into long, thin strips. Now bunch these strips together and cut them across into very small pieces – you should not work the fish into a very fine paste, but neither should it be too coarse, or it won't hold together. You should aim to achieve something in between.

2 Put the fish into a mixing bowl with the ginger, spring onions, mushrooms and some salt and pepper. Mix together well, then divide the mixture into 8 and, with slightly wet hands, shape into patties about 7.5 cm (3 inches) in diameter.

3 Heat a lightly oiled non-stick frying pan over a medium heat. Add the fishcakes, and fry for about 1½ minutes on each side until golden brown and cooked through. Put on to warmed plates and pile some of the rocket alongside. Whisk together the remaining ingredients to make a dressing and drizzle some over the rocket and a little around the outside edge of the plate.

I feel a very privileged sort of fellow to have gone fishing in a coracle for sea trout and, although not actually at my own hand, we caught a lovely four-pound fish that day in the Towy River, just downstream from Camarthen in Wales. I took it back to Raymond Reece's house filled with images of 'Under Milk Wood', since Raymond appeared to know half the people on whom Dylan Thomas modelled his characters in the poem. I must say that Camarthen, the Towy estuary and the little seaside village of Laugharne where Thomas lived were immeasurably romanticised for me by such characters as Captain Cat and Myfanwy Price, as we listened to a tape in the Land Rover on the way home again. We cooked the trout overlooking the river and served it with new potatoes and a hollandaise sauce made with sorrel from somebody's garden, and it didn't seem like a bad sort of day to be alive.

poached sea trout with sorrel hollandaise

SERVES 4

2 tablespoons sea salt
1 x 1.25–1.5 kg (2^1/$_2$–3 lb) sea trout, cleaned and scaled
Plain boiled potatoes (see page 194), to serve

FOR THE SORREL HOLLANDAISE:
4 tablespoons cold water
1 tablespoon white wine vinegar
1 teaspoon white peppercorns, crushed
225 g (8 oz) *Clarified butter* (see page 201)
15 g (^{1}/$_2$ oz) sorrel, large stalks removed
3 medium egg yolks
Juice of ^{1}/$_4$ small lemon
Pinch of cayenne pepper
Salt

1 Put 3.4 litres (6 pints) of water and the sea salt into a fish kettle and bring to the boil. Add the sea trout, making sure that the water covers it, then bring back to a simmer and poach gently for 16–18 minutes.

2 Lift the sea trout, resting on its trivet, out of the fish kettle and allow any excess water to drain away. Carefully lift it off the trivet with 2 fish slices and put it on a warmed serving plate. Remove the skin by making a shallow cut through the skin along the backbone and around the back of the head and carefully peeling it back, pulling out the fins as you get to them. Turn the fish over and repeat on the other side. Cover and keep warm.

3 For the sorrel hollandaise, bring the water, vinegar and crushed peppercorns to the boil in a small stainless-steel pan and simmer until reduced to about 2 tablespoons. Heat the clarified butter in a small pan and keep warm. Finely shred the sorrel leaves and then pass the knife through them so the shreds are roughly chopped.

4 Strain the reduction into a heatproof bowl, add the egg yolks and place the bowl over a pan of just-simmering water, making sure the base of the bowl is not touching the water. Whisk for about 4 minutes to create a soft, voluminous sabayon; it should become creamy and increase by about four times its volume. But don't allow the temperature of the sabayon to rise above 65°C (150°F), which will be uncomfortably hot when tested with your little finger.

5 Remove the bowl from the pan and gradually whisk in the warm clarified butter to make a thick emulsion. Whisk in the lemon juice, cayenne pepper, ¼ teaspoon of salt and the sorrel. Serve with the warm poached sea trout and boiled potatoes.

This must be made with fresh Kent cobnuts, which are harvested only for a few weeks in early autumn, from late August until the end of October – the same time as sprats are abundant (here in Padstow anyway). A very good cobnut producer who offers a mail-order service is Samantha Petter of Allens Farm, Plaxtol in Kent (tel: 01732 812215). I like cooking dishes that are in season, then leaving them alone for the rest of the year. But as Keith Floyd once said to me, after a long visit to Provence, where the French treat seasonal foods very seriously, 'You can get damn bored with flageolets after two weeks of nothing else.'

grilled sprats with cobnut 'pesto'

SERVES 4

16 sprats, cleaned and trimmed
A little sunflower oil for brushing
Salt and freshly ground black pepper

FOR THE COBNUT 'PESTO':
20 cobnuts, shelled
150 ml (5 fl oz) sunflower oil
The leaves from 1 sprig of marjoram
15 g ($^{1}/_{2}$ oz) parsley leaves
15 g ($^{1}/_{2}$ oz) Parmesan cheese, freshly grated
$^{1}/_{2}$ garlic clove
A few drops of lemon juice

1 For the cobnut pesto, put all the ingredients into a food processor and blend until smooth. Transfer to a bowl and season to taste.

2 Preheat the grill to high. Brush the sprats with a little sunflower oil and season on both sides with salt and pepper. Put them on a lightly oiled baking tray or the rack of the grill pan and cook for 1½–2 minutes on each side. Transfer to warmed plates and drizzle with the cobnut 'pesto'.

This is a spectacular dish, designed for eating outdoors on a hot summer's day. Aïoli is not a dish for eating at night, simply because you need the energetic digestion of the day to deal with the amount of garlic you will be eating. The classic accompaniments are salt cod, new potatoes and hardboiled eggs with whatever other seafood and vegetables you like. There are a lot of pots going on to the boil here, so if you find it quite tricky, pre-cook everything and serve it at room temperature or simply reheat the vegetables in boiling salted water just before serving. I like cooking everything fairly near to the time of serving and serving it all warm, rather than hot.

le grand aïoli

12 small uncooked beetroot, trimmed

450 g (1 lb) small new potatoes, scrubbed clean

2 globe artichokes

4 medium eggs

12 young carrots, trimmed

2 small bulbs of fennel, cut into wedges through the root

225 g (8 oz) fine green beans, trimmed

12 cooked Mediterranean crevettes

Maldon sea salt and coarsely crushed black pepper, to serve

FOR THE SALTED COD:

Plenty of cooking salt

450 g (1 lb) piece of thick, unskinned cod fillet, cut from the head end

2 bay leaves

1 onion, sliced

1 teaspoon black peppercorns

FOR THE AÏOLI:

8 garlic cloves, peeled

1 teaspoon salt

2 medium egg yolks

4 teaspoons lemon juice

350 ml (12 fl oz) extra virgin olive oil

1 Salt the cod the day before you want to serve the dish. Sprinkle a 1 cm (½ inch) thick layer of salt over the base of a plastic container. Put the piece of cod fillet on top, cover completely in another thick layer of salt and refrigerate overnight.

2 The next day, remove the cod from the brine and rinse it well under cold water. Cover with fresh cold water and leave to soak for 1 hour. Meanwhile, make a court-bouillon in which to cook the fish. Put the bay leaves, onion and peppercorns into a pan with 1.2 litres (2 pints) of water, bring to the boil and simmer for 20 minutes. Keep hot.

3 For the aïoli, crush the garlic cloves on a board with the salt, working them into a paste with the flat side of a large knife. Scoop the paste into a bowl, add the egg yolks and lemon juice and mix together briefly. Then very gradually whisk in the oil to make a thick, mayonnaise-like mixture. Spoon into a serving bowl and chill until needed.

4 When you are ready to assemble the dish, bring the court-bouillon back to the boil, add the salt cod and simmer for 12 minutes. Turn off the heat and set to one side to cool slightly in the liquid.

5 Put the beetroot and potatoes into separate pans of cold salted water, bring to the boil and simmer until tender. Drain well, peel the beetroot and set aside.

6 Trim the stalks of the artichokes and then cut each one lengthways into 6 wedges. Drop into a pan of boiling salted water, cover and cook for 15 minutes, then drain well. Scoop out the choke from each piece with a teaspoon. Return them to the pan, cover and keep warm. Hardboil the eggs for 8 minutes, then drain and cover with cold water. Set aside.

7 Drop the carrots into a pan of boiling salted water and simmer until tender. Lift out with a slotted spoon onto a plate, cover and keep warm. Add the fennel to the pan and cook for 4 minutes, then remove and set aside with the carrots. Add the green beans to the pan and cook for 3–4 minutes, until tender. Drain well.

8 To serve, arrange all the vegetables on one big platter. Shell and halve the eggs and arrange on another platter with the piece of warm salt cod and the crevettes. Serve with the bowl of aïoli and little bowls of Maldon salt and crushed black pepper.

There's a nice story attached to the naming of this classic French dish. The chef saucier of the Ritz in Paris, Monsieur Malley, left work after a busy lunch having instructed a young commis chef to add some tiny green Muscat grapes to the sole with white-wine sauce that was to be served that evening. On his return for service he discovered the young chef in a state of excitement; his young wife had just given birth to their first child, Véronique, and Monsieur Malley named the dish after her.

sole véronique

SERVES 4

8 x 75 g (3 oz) Dover sole fillets, skinned
600 ml (1 pint) *Fish stock* (see page 200),
or *Chicken stock* (see page 200)
85 ml (3 fl oz) dry vermouth,
such as Noilly Prat
300 ml (10 fl oz) double cream
A squeeze of lemon juice
25–30 seedless green grapes, preferably
Muscat, halved
Salt and freshly ground white pepper

FOR THE FLEURONS GARNISH:
250 g (9 oz) chilled puff pastry
A little flour, for rolling out
A little beaten egg, for glazing

1 For the fleurons, preheat the oven to 200°C/400°F/Gas Mark 6. Roll the pastry out thinly on a lightly floured surface and cut out eight 7.5 cm (3 inch) discs using a pastry cutter. Then, using the pastry cutter again, cut away one side of each disc to make a crescent-moon shape. Put on to a greased baking sheet and chill for 20 minutes. Then brush with beaten egg and with the tip of a small, sharp knife, lightly score a criss-cross pattern on each one. Bake for 20 minutes, or until puffed up and golden. Remove and keep warm. Lower the oven temperature to 180°C/350°F/Gas Mark 4.

2 Season the sole fillets lightly on both sides, then fold them in half, skinned-side innermost, and place side by side in a buttered shallow ovenproof dish. Pour over the fish stock, cover with foil and bake for 20 minutes.

3 Remove the fish from the dish and put on a warmed serving plate. Cover with foil and keep warm. Pour the cooking liquor into a saucepan, add the vermouth, then bring to the boil and boil vigorously until reduced to about 6 tablespoons. Add the cream and a squeeze of lemon juice and simmer until it has thickened to a coating consistency.

4 Add the grapes to the sauce and warm through gently. Season the sauce to taste, pour it over the fish and garnish with the puff pastry fleurons. Serve immediately.

I don't know where I learnt the technique of what I call close-cutting flat fish but it makes a world of difference to eating the whole fish. By cutting the lateral fins away from the fish very close to the underlying fillet, all those tiny bones that are so irritating when mixed with your potatoes are excluded.

I think this is one of the nicest ways of cooking flounder. It's not one of the best-flavoured flat fish but when served with a piquant sauce with lots of chopped herbs, onion, mustard and capers it's really rather good, especially at lunchtime. The fillets are coated in commercially produced Japanese 'panko' breadcrumbs made from slightly sweetened bread, which is what gives the fried coating such a crisp, golden finish. The crumbs are available from Chinese or Japanese supermarkets. I always think that less than prime cuts of meat and fish served with interesting sauces are the stuff of a good lunch, when one's appetite is keener and therefore takes more pleasure in things that at night would seem a little dull.

deep-fried flounder in panko crumbs with ravigote sauce

SERVES 4

4 x 350 g (12 oz) flounder, or other flat
fish such as lemon sole or plaice
Sunflower oil for deep-frying
50 g (2 oz) plain flour
2 medium eggs, beaten
100 g (4 oz) Japanese panko crumbs
Salt and freshly ground black pepper
Light green salad (see page 197) and
Chips (see page 194), to serve

FOR THE RAVIGOTE SAUCE:
4 teaspoons white wine vinegar
2 heaped teaspoons Dijon mustard
8–10 tablespoons olive oil
A good handful of mixed flat-leaf parsley,
tarragon and chervil leaves,
chopped
2 tablespoons chopped chives
A handful of watercress leaves,
roughly chopped
50 g (2 oz) finely chopped shallot
or onion
4 teaspoons *nonpareilles* capers,
drained and rinsed

1 Scale the fish if necessary (flounder have very small scales). Then cut off the frills and about 1 cm (½ inch) of the adjacent flesh with kitchen scissors, very close to the underlying fillet, to remove all the little lateral bones that run through the frills and part way into the fillet.

2 For the ravigote sauce, whisk together the vinegar and mustard, then gradually whisk in the oil. Stir in the chopped herbs, watercress leaves, shallot or onion, capers and some seasoning to taste. Set aside.

3 Heat some oil for deep-frying to 190°C/375°F. Season the fish lightly on both sides with salt and pepper and then coat in the flour, then in the egg and finally in the panko crumbs, pressing them on well to give a good, even coating. Deep-fry for 4 minutes, until crisp, golden and cooked through. Drain briefly on kitchen paper and keep warm in a low oven while you cook the rest of the fish. Then transfer to warmed plates and serve with the ravigote sauce and the green salad and chips.

FISH AND SHELLFISH DEEP-FRIED FLOUNDER IN PANKO CRUMBS

Paul Flynn of the Tannery Restaurant in Dungarvan, near Cork, is a bit of a food hero of mine. A local boy, he went to London to cook with some of the great chefs, including Nico Ladenis. But rather than continue in the metropolis, he decided to go home and has put this rather sleepy but charming seaside town on the gastronomic map. I say this because when you drive in now, there are signs everywhere saying 'To the Tannery Restaurant'. Paul sent the recipe over with this introduction: 'I am making this restaurant style because for dinner parties, it's so much easier. The idea is that all your vegetables have been pre-cooked and refreshed. This can be done earlier in the day, leaving you calm and serene. The sauce can be done beforehand too, so that at the end it's really just an assembly job.'

bourride of monkfish and mussels

SERVES 4

450 g (1 lb) mussels, cleaned (see page 74)

A splash of dry white wine

12 small new potatoes, scrubbed clean

1 leek, cut into slices 1 cm ($1/2$ inch) thick

50–75 g (2–3 oz) mangetout or fine green beans, trimmed

1 x 500 g (1 lb 2 oz) prepared monkfish tail

12 cherry tomatoes

4 spring onions, cut into 2.5 cm (1 inch) lengths

2 tablespoons chopped chives

2 baby Cos lettuce, leaves separated

Salt and freshly ground black pepper

FOR THE GARLIC CREAM SAUCE:

A large handful of thyme sprigs

300 ml (10 fl oz) double cream

5 shallots, peeled

10 garlic cloves, peeled

3 tablespoons warm melted butter

2 teaspoons lemon juice

1 For the garlic cream sauce, tie the thyme into a bunch and wrap it in muslin. Pour the cream into a saucepan, add the thyme and bring to the boil. Remove from the heat and leave to infuse for about 1 hour.

2 Meanwhile, preheat the oven to 180°C/350°F/Gas Mark 4. Pile the shallots and garlic into the centre of a sheet of foil, bring the edges up slightly and pour over the melted butter. Seal into a parcel, place on a baking sheet and roast for 1 hour, until the shallots and garlic are very soft. Undo the parcel, lift the shallots and garlic out of the buttery juices and put them into a liquidiser.

3 Remove the thyme from the cream and squeeze well to extract all the flavour. Add the cream to the liquidiser with the shallots and garlic and blend to a smooth purée, then press through a sieve into a large, clean pan.

4 Heat a pan over a high heat. Add the mussels and wine, cover with a lid and cook for 2–3 minutes, until the mussels have just opened, but don't overcook them. Tip them into a colander set over a bowl to collect the juices. When they are cool enough to handle, remove the mussels from all but a few of the smaller shells. Add 85 ml (3 fl oz) of the mussel cooking liquor to the garlic cream sauce and simmer until reduced to a good coating consistency. Season to taste with the lemon juice and some salt and pepper.

5 Cook the potatoes in well-salted water until tender, then drain and set aside. Drop the leek into a pan of boiling salted water and cook for 2 minutes, until just tender. Lift out with a slotted spoon and refresh under cold water, then leave to drain. Add the mangetout or green beans to the pan and cook until just tender. Drain, refresh and set aside with the leek.

6 Shortly before serving, trim away all the membrane from the monkfish tail and cut it across, through the bone, into slices 2 cm (¾ inch) thick. Bring the sauce to a simmer, add the monkfish slices and simmer gently for 3 minutes. Add the potatoes and cherry tomatoes and simmer for 1 minute. Then add the leek, mangetout or beans, and spring onions, bring back to a simmer and cook for 1 minute. Stir in the mussels, adjust the seasoning if necessary, and then stir in most of the chives.

7 Divide the lettuce leaves between 4 warmed, deep, bistro-style plates. Spoon in the stew and sprinkle with the remaining chives.

Chinese seafood cooking is some of the best in the world. It never ceases to amaze me how rarely one comes into contact with it. Most Chinese restaurants seem to adopt a policy of one menu for Westerners and one for them. I've been into restaurants in Soho, London, with chef friends who have explained patiently to the staff, 'No, we don't want what's on the menu, we want proper Chinese food', and mysteriously, lovely dishes of clams fragrant with coriander, aromatic stews with star anise and tangerine peel, and beautiful, delicately steamed fish appear. The problem is not unique to this country. I recall seeing a message printed in Chinese in an Australian food magazine designed to be torn out and taken with you, which ran something like, 'I'm not one of your ignorant Westerners. Please give me some proper Chinese food.' Occasionally though, with restaurants like the Mandarin Kitchen in London, or the restaurant where I had this in Glasgow, Ho Wong, they do give you the real thing, and those places are always packed with grateful *guilos*.

steamed monkfish with wild garlic and ginger

SERVES 2

350–400 g (12–14 oz) monkfish fillet
¹/₂ tablespoon very finely shredded fresh ginger
A small bunch of wild garlic (about 4 leaves), or a small bunch of garlic chives, or 1 garlic clove, cut into fine shreds
1 teaspoon sesame oil
1 tablespoon dark soy sauce
2 spring onions, thinly sliced on the diagonal
Salt
Steamed rice (see page 198), to serve

1 Lightly season the monkfish fillet with salt and then cut it across into thin slices. Arrange the slices in a single layer over a heatproof serving plate and scatter over the ginger.

2 Put some sort of trivet in a wide, shallow pan, add 1 cm (½ inch) of water and bring to the boil. Rest the plate on the trivet, cover the pan with a well-fitting lid and steam for 2–3 minutes, until the fish is almost cooked.

3 Scatter the wild garlic, garlic chives or shredded fresh garlic over the fish and steam, covered, for a further minute. Meanwhile, put the sesame oil and soy sauce into a small pan and heat briefly.

4 Remove the fish from the steamer and pour away about half the cooking juices. Scatter over the spring onions, pour over the hot sesame oil and soy mixture and serve with some steamed rice.

I picked up the idea for this recipe on a recent trip to Sydney and a visit to the MG Garage Restaurant. The chef, Jeremy Stroud, is one of quite a large number of English cooks who have made their name in Australia. Interestingly, there is almost an equal number of Australian chefs who have made their name over here. I like this dish because it takes three very simple ideas – a pan-fried fillet of fish like John Dory, a potato boulangère and a few sautéed wild mushrooms – and in bringing them together creates a whole that is greater than the sum of its parts. I think that John Dory is particularly suited to pan-frying. I get heartily fed up with more oily fish like salmon that has been pan-fried more or less totally on the skin-side and comes to the table blackened and reeking of what cottages in Cornwall must have smelt like when they used pilchard oil in their lamps.

pan-fried john dory with thyme boulangère potatoes and mushrooms

SERVES 4

15 g (¹/₂ oz) dried porcini mushrooms
225 g (8 oz) mixed fresh mushrooms,
such as girolles, portobello, chestnut
and button
1 tablespoon sunflower oil
40 g (1¹/₂ oz) unsalted butter
2 x 675 g (1¹/₂ lb) John Dory, filleted
The leaves from 1 small sprig of thyme
Salt and freshly ground black pepper

FOR THE THYME BOULANGÈRE POTATOES:
900 ml (1¹/₂ pints) *Chicken stock*
(see page 200)
50 g (2 oz) butter
The leaves from 4 sprigs of thyme
900 g (2 lb) floury potatoes, such as
Maris Piper, peeled and cut into slices
5 mm (¹/₄ inch) thick
1 small onion, thinly sliced

1 Cover the dried porcini with hot water and leave them to soak for 20 minutes, then drain and slice them thinly. For the thyme boulangère potatoes, put the chicken stock into a pan and boil rapidly until reduced by half. Add the butter, thyme leaves, ½ teaspoon of salt and some pepper and, when the butter has melted, add the sliced potatoes and onion. Bring to a simmer and cook gently for about 5 minutes, until the potatoes are just tender when pierced with a knife.

2 Preheat the oven to 200°C/400°F/Gas Mark 6. Lightly butter a 1.5 litre (2½ pint) shallow baking dish. Layer the potatoes and onions in the dish, finishing the top layer neatly if you wish. Pour over the remaining stock, cover loosely with foil and bake for 45–50 minutes.

3 Wipe or brush any dirt from the fresh mushrooms and slice them into even-sized pieces. When the potatoes are nearly cooked, heat the oil and 15 g (½ oz) of the butter in a large frying pan. Season the John Dory fillets on both sides, add to the pan skin-side down and fry over a medium-high heat for 2 minutes on each side. Lift on to a plate and keep warm.

4 Add the remaining butter to the frying pan, add the fresh and soaked porcini mushrooms, thyme leaves and some seasoning and fry briskly over a high heat for 2 minutes, until tender.

5 Remove the boulangère potatoes from the oven and divide between 4 warmed plates. Place the John Dory fillets on top and spoon the mushrooms alongside.

This has become a bit of a modern classic and, typically for me, when my chum, Bill Baker, served it up for lunch one day I excitedly said, 'Where on earth did this come from? It's so good.' And then discovered that every chef I respect knew about it, and had it regularly on their menus, including Rowley Leigh of Kensington Place and Brian Turner of Brian Turner Mayfair in Grosvenor Square.

It seems to me the perfect way to serve smoked eel – apart, that is from just sliced with lemon wedges and brown bread and butter. I have to say, there is rather a lot of second-rate smoked eel around, with a noticeable taste of pond water, and I would highly recommend Frank Hederman's smoked eel from Belvelly Smokehouse, Cobh, County Cork, Eire (tel: 00 353 21 4811089).

smoked-eel and bacon salad with pink fir apple potatoes

SERVES 4

350 g (12 oz) Pink Fir Apple potatoes, scrubbed clean
225 g (8 oz) smoked eel fillet
2 teaspoons sunflower oil
12 rashers of rindless dry-cured streaky bacon
175 g (6 oz) mixed baby salad leaves
4 spring onions, sliced on the diagonal
1 tablespoon extra virgin olive oil
2 tablespoons chopped chives
Salt and freshly ground black pepper

FOR THE DRESSING:

1 tablespoon white wine vinegar
A good pinch of caster sugar
$2^1/_2$ teaspoons finely grated horseradish (from a jar)
1 tablespoon double cream
1 tablespoon finely chopped flat-leaf parsley

1 Put the potatoes into a pan of well-salted water (1 teaspoon salt per 600 ml/1 pint water), bring to the boil and simmer for 12 minutes or until just tender. Meanwhile, cut the smoked eel fillet in half lengthways and then across into pieces 10 cm (4 inches) long. Mix together all the ingredients for the dressing and season to taste with some salt and pepper.

2 Heat 1 teaspoon of the oil in a heavy-based frying pan, add half the bacon rashers in a single layer and fry for 4–5 minutes, turning once, until crisp and richly golden. Remove from the pan and keep warm. Repeat with the rest of the rashers.

3 Drain the potatoes and cut them across into slices. Toss the salad leaves and spring onions in a bowl with the olive oil and a little seasoning.

4 Divide the salad leaves between 4 plates and tuck the pieces of eel, the potato slices and the bacon rashers in amongst them. Drizzle over the dressing and sprinkle with the chopped chives. Serve while the potatoes are still warm.

The idea of conger-eel soup with marigold petals didn't appeal to me. It sounded like very 'arty' local food, invented to give weight to Jersey culture. In fact it was very good, mostly because the baker, David Dodge, whose version of it is a long-established recipe, cooked it so well. The secret lies in adding the peas and cabbage right at the end, and using plenty of thyme. I'm not sure that the marigold petals taste of much, but they look appealing.

conger eel soup with peas, thyme and marigold petals

SERVES 6

2–3 tablespoons olive oil
75 g (3 oz) butter
100 g (4 oz) shallots, finely chopped
200 g (7 oz) young leeks, sliced
$^1/_2$ small Savoy cabbage, thinly sliced
1 teaspoon thyme leaves
200 g (7 oz) fresh peas
A large bunch of flat-leaf parsley, roughly chopped
About 1litre (1$^3/_4$ pints) full-cream milk
Salt and freshly ground white pepper
Marigold petals, if available, to garnish
Crusty fresh bread, to serve

FOR THE STOCK:

1 kg (2$^1/_4$ lb) fresh conger eel (head, bones and tail) thoroughly washed
2–3 fresh bay leaves
1 teaspoon white peppercorns
2–3 carrots, thinly sliced
3–4 celery sticks, sliced
2–3 leeks, sliced
A bouquet garni of thyme sprigs and parsley stalks

1 To make the stock, put the conger eel head, bones and tail into a large pan with the bay leaves and peppercorns and add just enough water to barely cover. Bring to the boil, then cover and simmer gently for 30 minutes, without stirring but occasionally skimming any scum from the surface. Add the vegetables and herbs 5–10 minutes before the stock has finished cooking. Drain through a fine sieve and leave until cool enough to handle. Flake the fish from the bones and set aside for finishing the soup.

2 For the soup, heat the pan over a high heat, then add the olive oil, lower the heat to medium and add the butter, shallots and leeks. Cook for 5 minutes or so, until the vegetables have softened, then add the conger eel stock. Increase the heat to high and bring to the boil, then add the cabbage and a little salt and simmer for a few minutes.

3 Add the thyme and peas and simmer for a few minutes longer, until the vegetables are just cooked. Add the reserved conger eel flesh, parsley and sufficient milk to give the soup a pleasing consistency. Remove from the heat just before it boils and adjust the seasoning. Serve in warmed bowls, scattered with a few marigold petals if you have them, and accompanied by some crusty bread.

In Cumbria, of all places, there is a very intelligent and committed Sri Lankan woman called Manel Trepte who runs a company called Demel's Sri Lankan Chutneys in Ulverston (tel: 01229 861012). Using recipes from her home country, she makes chutneys and fresh pickles that have an astounding clarity and purity of taste. One of the reasons for this, she thinks, is that she doesn't use onion in any of her products, as she believes it would overpower them. You feel as if you are tasting every element of the chutneys. While I was filming there, she knocked up this little dish for lunch. Fragrant and fresh, it's a perfect recipe to use for farmed salmon. Interestingly, she says that in southern India and Sri Lanka spices are not roasted for fish curries, giving a more delicate flavour to the dish.

sri lankan fish curry

SERVES 4

A walnut-sized piece of tamarind pulp
4 x 225 g (8 oz) salmon steaks
2 tablespoons sunflower oil
1 large onion, chopped
4 garlic cloves, finely chopped
8 fresh curry leaves
2 small pieces rampe (screwpine), optional
1/2 teaspoon ground turmeric
1 teaspoon chilli powder
2 tomatoes, skinned and chopped
400 ml (14 fl oz) can of coconut milk
Salt
Steamed rice (see page 198) and Asian-style chutneys such as mango, lime, aubergine or tamarind, to serve

FOR THE SRI LANKAN CURRY POWDER:
2¹/2 tablespoons coriander seeds
1 tablespoon cumin seeds
1¹/2 teaspoons fennel seeds
A pinch of fenugreek seeds
2.5 cm (1 inch) piece of cinnamon stick
3 cloves
2 green cardamom pods
6 black peppercorns

1 For the Sri Lankan curry powder, simply grind everything together to a fine powder in a spice grinder. Store in a screw-top jar.

2 Put the tamarind pulp into a small bowl with 85 ml (3 fl oz) warm water. Work the pulp into the water with your fingers until it has broken down and the seeds have been released. Strain the slightly syrupy liquid through a fine sieve into another bowl and discard the fibrous mixture left in the sieve.

3 Rinse the fish steaks under cold water and dry on kitchen paper. Heat the oil in a large, shallow pan, add the onion, garlic, curry leaves and rampe, if using, and fry gently for 7–10 minutes, until the onion is soft and lightly golden.

4 Add the turmeric, chilli powder and 2 tablespoons of the Sri Lankan curry powder and fry for 1–2 minutes. Add the tomatoes, tamarind liquid, coconut milk and 1 teaspoon of salt and simmer gently for 15 minutes.

5 Add the salmon steaks to the pan and spoon some of the sauce over them. Simmer gently for 5 minutes, then cover the pan and set aside for 30 minutes. By this time the fish should be cooked through – but if not, just return it to the heat for a few minutes. Serve with some steamed rice and the chutneys.

David Pritchard, who makes all my television programmes and is a thoroughly good cook (apart from a predilection for Bisto, which I find incomprehensible), brought this recipe, or something very similar, back from Benidorm. He has cooked it many times for the television crew for lunch, which we enjoy with lots of hearty red wine such as the Rioja, Marques de Caceres. I actually prefer it to paella because the enduring problem with paella is that some of the ingredients are always overcooked. Arroz a la banda, which means 'rice served apart', allows for the rice and seafood to be cooked and served separately – to me, a much better arrangement, especially when accompanied by a searing-hot garlic allioli.

The recipe makes just a small amount of this exceptionally pungent sauce, and a teaspoon or so is all you will need per person, just like mustard. If you favour something less demanding, try the recipe for *Aïoli* instead on page 58. I have purposely written this recipe using ingredients you can get anywhere, except perhaps for the smoked paprika called La Chinata. The rich fish stock uses small, cheap fish such as gurnard or whiting, or steaks of bigger fish. If I'm making this in Cornwall, I'll bung in a few shore crabs, prawns or lobster shells, too, to add flavour.

arroz a la banda (saffron rice and squid served with allioli)

SERVES 4

2 tablespoons extra virgin olive oil
2 good pinches of paprika
450 g (1 lb) cleaned squid, cut across into rings and the tentacles cut into
7.5 cm (3 inch) pieces
Salt and freshly ground black pepper

1 First make an aromatic fish stock to flavour the rice. Heat the olive oil in a large pan, add the garlic, chilli flakes and orange zest and fry until the garlic is just beginning to colour. Add the onion, red pepper and fennel and fry until soft. Now add the fish and tomatoes and continue to fry for 5 minutes or so, stirring occasionally.

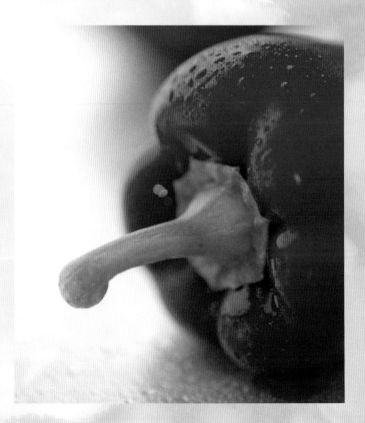

FOR THE FISH STOCK:

4 tablespoons olive oil

4 garlic cloves, sliced (no need to peel)

A large pinch of dried chilli flakes

2 strips of pared orange zest

1 onion, sliced

1 red pepper, sliced (no need to seed)

1 fennel bulb, sliced

675 g (1½ lb) cheap, but well-flavoured small fish, such as gurnard, cleaned but left whole, OR steaks or fillets of fish such as ling and pollack, cut into slightly smaller pieces

2 tomatoes, sliced

1.5 litres (2½ pints) water

A small handful of oregano leaves

A large pinch of saffron strands

FOR THE RICE:

2 tablespoons extra virgin olive oil

1½ teaspoons paprika

A large pinch of smoked paprika, preferably La Chinata (optional)

2 garlic cloves, finely chopped

500 g (1 lb 2 oz) paella rice or risotto rice

FOR THE ALLIOLI:

25 g (1 oz) garlic, finely chopped

85 ml (3 fl oz) extra virgin olive oil

2 Add the water and oregano and bring to the boil. Reduce the heat and simmer for 40 minutes, then strain the stock. The best piece of equipment to use for straining a rich stock like this is a conical strainer, as it allows you to force as much flavour as possible through with the back of a ladle. If you don't have one, press the cooked fish and vegetables against the side of a sieve. Add the saffron and ½ teaspoon of salt to the stock, set aside and keep hot.

3 For the rice, heat the oil in a shallow pan in which you can serve it (I use a shallow Le Creuset casserole, 30 cm/12 inches in diameter), with the paprika, the smoked paprika, if using, and the garlic. As soon as the garlic starts to colour, add the rice and stir-fry for about 2 minutes. Add the hot stock, 1 teaspoon of salt and some black pepper and bring to the boil, stirring occasionally. Reduce the heat a little and cook, uncovered, without stirring, for 8 minutes. Then reduce the heat right down to low and cook for a further 7 minutes, again without stirring. Now test the rice; it should still have a slight bite to it. Remove the pan from the heat, cover and leave for 5 minutes. When you take the lid off, the rice should look marvellous – each grain separate and the top an appetising yellow-brown with flecks of saffron.

4 While the rice is cooking, make the allioli: pound the garlic and ½ teaspoon of salt in a mortar, then mix in the oil a little at a time to build up an emulsion (it won't be as stable as mayonnaise but will taste almost as fierce as chilli sauce). Transfer to a small bowl.

5 To cook the squid, heat the olive oil in a large frying pan. Toss in a pinch of paprika and half the squid and fry over a high heat for 2 minutes, until lightly coloured. Season with salt, remove and repeat with the remaining squid. Serve the rice with the stir-fried squid and allioli.

FISH AND SHELLFISH ARROZ A LA BANDA

71

This is another modern classic, wildly popular in Australia but not so well known here. The secret of success lies in getting the thinnest possible tempura batter and a good combination of chilli in a crunchy salad – in this case, beansprouts and watercress.

salt and pepper squid tempura with coriander

SERVES 4

450 g (1 lb) cleaned medium-sized squid

Sunflower oil for deep-frying

A large handful of small
coriander sprigs

25 g (1 oz) fresh beansprouts

A large handful of watercress sprigs

2 medium-hot red Dutch chillies,
seeded and thinly sliced

1 teaspoon dark soy sauce

FOR THE SALT AND PEPPER TEMPURA BATTER:

1 teaspoon black peppercorns

1 teaspoon Sichuan peppercorns

50 g (2 oz) plain flour

50 g (2 oz) cornflour

A big pinch of Chinese five-spice powder

1 teaspoon Maldon sea salt

175 ml (6 fl oz) ice-cold soda water,
from a new bottle

1 Insert the blade of a sharp, thin knife into the opening of each squid body pouch and slit it open along one side. Open it out flat, cut it lengthways into strips 1 cm (½ inch) wide, and then cut them in half into shorter strips.

2 For the batter, put the black and Sichuan peppercorns into a mortar and grind coarsely. Sift the flour and cornflour into a bowl and stir in the crushed peppercorns, five-spice powder and Maldon salt. Stir in the soda water until only just mixed; the batter should still be a little lumpy, very thin and almost transparent. If it seems a bit thick, add a drop more water.

3 Heat some oil for deep-frying to 190°C/375°F. Dip the pieces of squid into the batter a few at a time and deep-fry for 1 minute, until crisp and golden. Transfer to a baking tray lined with kitchen paper and keep hot in a low oven while you cook the rest.

4 Mix together the coriander sprigs, beansprouts and watercress and divide between 4 plates. Sprinkle over the red chillies, then tuck the pieces of squid in amongst the leaves. Sprinkle lightly with the soy sauce and serve immediately.

This is the Italian version of fish pie. Unusually for fish dishes, it tastes just as good when reheated. You can, of course, put any type of seafood in a lasagne and add mussels, clams or squid but I find that in the baking the mussels become very fishy tasting and the squid tough. For me, the perfect combination is a flaky white fish, those sweet, pink North Atlantic prawns and white crab meat. The New Zealand fish hoki is ideal for this dish, being white and firm-fleshed. Strange I should be recommending a foreign fish, but it is accredited by the Marine Stewardship Council, in other words it is from a sustainable fishery.

seafood lasagne

SERVES 8

550 g (1¼ lb) hoki, ling, cod, coley or
pollack fillets, skinned

250 g (9 oz) (12 sheets) fresh lasagne

175 g (6 oz) peeled North
Atlantic prawns

225 g (8 oz) fresh white crab meat

Salt and freshly ground black pepper

1 For the tomato sauce, heat the oil in a pan, add the onions and garlic and cook gently until softened. Add the tomatoes and simmer gently for 15–20 minutes, stirring now and then, until reduced and thickened. Put the vinegar and sugar into a small pan and boil rapidly until reduced to 2 teaspoons. Stir into the tomato sauce and season to taste with salt and pepper. Stir in the basil and set aside.

FOR THE TOMATO SAUCE:
4 tablespoons olive oil
2 onions, finely chopped
2 garlic cloves, finely chopped
2 x 400 g (14 oz) cans of
chopped tomatoes
100 ml (3¹/₂ fl oz) red wine vinegar
4 teaspoons caster sugar
A large handful of basil leaves,
thinly shredded

FOR THE BÉCHAMEL SAUCE:
1 large onion, peeled and halved
6 cloves
1.2 litres (2 pints) full-cream milk
2 bay leaves
1 teaspoon black peppercorns
65 g (2¹/₂ oz) butter
65 g (2¹/₂ oz) plain flour
4 tablespoons double cream
50 g (2 oz) Parmesan cheese,
freshly grated

2 For the béchamel sauce, stud the onion with the cloves and put it into a pan with the milk, bay leaves and peppercorns. Bring to the boil and then set aside for 20 minutes to infuse.

3 Bring the milk back to the boil, add the fish fillets and simmer for 8 minutes. Lift the fish on to a plate and strain the milk into a jug. When cool enough to handle, break it into large flakes, discarding any bones.

4 Bring a large pan of well-salted water to the boil (1 teaspoon salt per 600 ml/1 pint water). Drop in the sheets of lasagne, one at a time, take the pan off the heat and leave them to soak for 5 minutes. Drain well and set aside.

5 To finish the béchamel sauce, melt the butter in a non-stick pan, add the flour and cook over a medium heat for 1 minute. Lower the heat and gradually beat in the milk, then bring to the boil, stirring. Simmer gently over a low heat for 10 minutes, giving it a stir every now and then. Remove the pan from the heat and stir in the cream, half the Parmesan cheese and some seasoning to taste.

6 Preheat the oven to 200°C/400°F/Gas Mark 6. To assemble the lasagne, arrange a layer of the pasta over the base of a 3.4 litre (6 pint) shallow ovenproof dish. Spoon over half the tomato sauce and then scatter over half the flaked white fish, prawns and crab meat. Spoon over one third of the béchamel sauce and then repeat the layers once more. Finish with a final layer of the pasta and the remaining béchamel sauce. The lasagne can be prepared in advance to this stage; cover and chill until needed.

7 If the lasagne has been chilled for some time, allow it to come back to room temperature before baking. Sprinkle over the remaining Parmesan cheese and bake for 40–50 minutes, until golden and bubbling.

Funnily enough, I haven't done a recipe for moules marinière for ages – not since my first book, *English Seafood Cookery*, published by Penguin in 1986. I was leafing through a new BBC poetry book, *The Nation's Favourite Poems of Desire*, and I came across a poem by Elizabeth Garrett that subtly ties together the sensuality of eating mussels with your fingers. She describes cooking the mussels as follows:

'I pour on wine; it seems they beg for more,
The beaked shells yearning wide as if in song –
Yet dumb – and lewdly lolling parrot-tongues.
Cream licks the back of a spoon and drawls a slur
Of unctuous benediction for this feast.
We smooth our cassocks; bow our heads; and eat.'

moules marinière with cream, garlic and parsley

SERVES 4

1.75 kg (4 lb) mussels
1 garlic clove, finely chopped
2 shallots, finely chopped
15 g ($^1/_2$ oz) butter
A bouquet garni of parsley, thyme and bay leaves
100 ml ($3^1/_2$ fl oz) dry white wine
120 ml (4 fl oz) double cream
A handful of parsley leaves, coarsely chopped
Crusty bread, to serve

1 Wash the mussels under plenty of cold running water. Discard any open ones that won't close when lightly squeezed. Pull out the tough, fibrous beards protruding from between the tightly closed shells and then knock off any barnacles with a large knife and give the mussels another quick rinse to remove any little pieces of shell.

2 Soften the garlic and shallots in the butter with the bouquet garni, in a large pan big enough to take all the mussels – it should only be half full. Add the mussels and wine, turn up the heat, then cover and steam them open in their own juices for 3–4 minutes, giving the pan a good shake every now and then.

3 Remove the bouquet garni, add the cream and parsley and remove from the heat. Spoon into 4 large warmed bowls and serve with lots of crusty bread.

I have been very keen in this book to make sure that all the ingredients for the recipes are easy to get hold of because, unlike the first volume of *Food Heroes*, it doesn't include a list of specialist suppliers (instead they have been covered in the companion volume to this book, *Guide to the Food Heroes of Britain*). However, I have made an exception with razor clams because I like them so much, and have listed a couple of suppliers at the end of this recipe from whom you can get them mail order. Funnily enough, you are more likely to find razor clams in Chinese restaurants than in fish shops. The Chinese really know their seafood. I recently had a banquet for my family in a good Chinese restaurant in London where a single razor clam, cooked this way, was served as a first course. It was delicious, but quite tricky to eat such a long, thin clam with chopsticks. For this reason I've cut the clams up here but I still think they should be served on top of a few of the shells.

stir-fried razor clams with black beans and chilli

SERVES 2

8 large or 12 small razor clams
2 tablespoons Chinese rice wine
2 teaspoons Chinese salted fermented black beans
A good pinch of caster sugar
1 tablespoon sunflower oil
2 teaspoons sesame oil
2 garlic cloves, finely chopped
1 cm (^{1}/$_2$ inch) piece of fresh ginger, peeled and finely chopped
^{1}/$_2$ medium-hot Dutch red chilli, thinly sliced
1 teaspoon dark soy sauce
8 spring onions, thinly sliced on the diagonal
Steamed rice (see page 198), to serve

1 If the clams are sandy, wash them in plenty of cold water and drain well. Place a large sauté pan or frying pan over a high heat. When it is hot, add the clams and the Chinese rice wine, then cover and cook for 2–3 minutes, until the clams have just opened. Remove the clams from the pan and discard the cooking juices. Remove the meats from the shells and cut each one on the diagonal into 3 or 4 pieces. Discard all but 4 of the shells.

2 Put the black beans on a board, sprinkle over the sugar and chop them coarsely. Heat the sunflower and sesame oils in the pan, add the black beans, garlic and ginger and stir-fry for 20 seconds. Return the clams to the pan with the chilli and stir-fry for 1 minute, until nicely coloured. Add the soy sauce and most of the spring onions and toss together briefly.

3 Put 2 clam shells on each warmed plate and spoon the stir-fried clams on top. Sprinkle with the remaining spring onions and then serve, with some steamed rice if you wish.

FOR RAZOR CLAMS BY MAIL ORDER:
Matthew Stevens & Son, Back Road East, St Ives, Cornwall TR26 1NW (tel: 01736 799392). www.mstevensandson.com
Andy Race Fish Merchants, The Harbour, Port of Mallaig, Inverness-shire, PH41 4PX (tel: 01687 462626). www.andyrace.co.uk

FISH AND SHELLFISH STIR-FRIED RAZOR CLAMS

I've had a lot of success serving scallops grilled in their shells; I think the aroma of hot shells adds a lot of excitement. I've never had a dish like this in Mexico, but I'd love to. Using pumpkin seeds to thicken a sauce or a dressing is very popular there, as is the combination of green chilli and coriander.

grilled scallops with pumpkin seed, serrano chilli and coriander sauce

SERVES 4

50 g (2 oz) pumpkin seeds
1 serrano (hot green) chilli, chopped
A large handful (about 25 g/1 oz) coriander leaves
2 garlic cloves, peeled
150 ml (5 fl oz) sunflower oil
Juice of 1 lime
2 spring onions, chopped
7 g ($^1/_4$ oz) Parmesan cheese, freshly grated
16–20 cleaned king scallops in the shell or 32 cleaned queen scallops
25 g (1 oz) butter, melted
Salt

1 For the sauce, put the pumpkin seeds, chilli, coriander, garlic, oil, lime juice, spring onions, Parmesan cheese and ½ teaspoon of salt into a food processor and blend to a smooth paste.

2 Preheat the grill to high. Put the scallops on to a baking tray, brush each one generously with melted butter and season with salt and pepper. Grill the king scallops for 2 minutes and the queen scallops for 1 minute.

3 Lightly spread about 1 teaspoon of the pumpkin-seed sauce over the scallops (use about ½ teaspon for the 'queenies') and grill for another 1–2 minutes (1 minute for the queenies) until they are just cooked through and the sauce has just started to colour. Place on 4 warmed plates and serve straight away.

The secret of success when making this recipe lies in cooking the oysters very lightly, and getting a lovely voluminous softness to the sabayon. It's not an easy recipe, I have to admit, but it's a triumph when you get it right.

oyster and spinach tarts with a vermouth sabayon

SERVES 6

1 quantity *Rich shortcrust pastry*
(see page 201)
12 large or 18 smaller Pacific oysters
450 g (1 lb) baby leaf spinach
15 g (¹/₂ oz) butter
Salt and freshly ground black pepper
A little watercress, to garnish

FOR THE VERMOUTH SABAYON:
2 tablespoons Noilly Prat, or similar white vermouth
2 teaspoons white wine vinegar
12 white peppercorns, finely crushed
3 medium egg yolks
100 g (4 oz) *Clarified butter* (see page 201)
A few drops of lemon juice

1 Cut the pastry into 6 even-sized pieces. Roll out on a lightly floured surface and use to line 6 greased 10 cm (4 inch) loose-bottomed tartlet tins. Prick the bases with a fork and chill for 20 minutes.

2 Preheat the oven to 200°C/400°F/Gas Mark 6. Line the tartlet cases with greaseproof paper and a thin layer of baking beans and bake for 15 minutes. Remove the paper and beans and bake for a further 5 minutes. Remove and lower the oven temperature to 160°C/325°F/Gas Mark 3.

3 Open the oysters, retaining as much of their liquid as you can. Release them from their shells, tip them into a sieve set over a bowl and leave to drain.

4 Wash the spinach and remove the excess water – a salad spinner does this brilliantly. Heat a large pan over a high heat, add the butter and the spinach, cover and cook gently until the spinach has wilted right down. Remove the lid and continue to cook until any excess moisture has disappeared. Season very lightly with a little salt and pepper.

5 For the sabayon, put the vermouth, vinegar, crushed white peppercorns and 80 ml (3 fl oz) of the oyster liquor into a small pan and leave to bubble over a medium-high heat until it has reduced to 3 tablespoons. Pour this reduction into a large, heatproof bowl and leave to cool.

6 Remove the pastry cases from their tins and put them on a baking tray. Spoon the spinach into the base of each tartlet case and top with the oysters. Lay a large sheet of well-buttered greaseproof paper over the top of the tarts and put them into the oven for 7–8 minutes to heat through and lightly set the oysters.

7 Meanwhile, add the egg yolks to the reduction, place the bowl over a pan of simmering water and whisk vigorously until the mixture is thick, light and frothy and leaves a trail over the surface. Remove the bowl from the heat and whisk in the clarified butter and lemon juice.

8 Preheat the grill to high. Remove the tarts from the oven and take off the greaseproof paper. Spoon over the sabayon and place under the grill for about 30 seconds, until lightly browned. Transfer the tarts to warmed plates and garnish with a little watercress. Serve straight away.

There's no reason why we shouldn't be able to get freshwater crayfish because our rivers are teeming with them. About twenty years ago an American species was inadvertently let loose in a river, and in that short time they have colonised much of the country and destroyed our indigenous species, a bit like grey and red squirrels. Fortunately they are delicious and abundant, and can be caught as easily as shore crabs from a harbour wall simply by dangling some meat or fish into the river and pulling them up as they grab at it. If you can't get them though, this dish works equally well with langoustines, lobster or large raw prawns. In both cases, cook them in well-salted water to bring out the flavour.

linguine with freshwater crayfish, tomatoes, basil and cream

SERVES 2

2 kg (4 lb) live freshwater crayfish or
225 g (8 oz) cooked freshwater
crayfish tail meat
225 g (8 oz) dried linguine
2 tablespoons extra virgin olive oil
2 garlic cloves, finely chopped
4 vine-ripened tomatoes, skinned,
seeded and roughly chopped
50 ml (2 fl oz) dry white wine
2–3 tablespoons double cream
1 small bunch of basil, torn into
small pieces
Salt and freshly ground black pepper

1 If you are using live freshwater crayfish, bring a large pan of well-salted water to the boil (1 teaspoon salt per 600 ml/1 pint water), add the crayfish, bring back to the boil and cook for 2 minutes. Drain and leave until cool enough to handle. Peel by breaking off and discarding the heads, pinching the tail shell between your thumb and forefinger until it cracks and then breaking the shell apart along the underbelly and removing the flesh – much as you would for langoustines.

2 Bring another pan of well-salted water to the boil. Add the linguine and cook for 8–9 minutes, until *al dente*.

3 Meanwhile, heat the olive oil in a shallow pan, add the garlic and, as soon as it starts to sizzle, add the tomatoes, white wine and some seasoning. Cook for 4–5 minutes, until the tomatoes have reduced and thickened slightly. Add the crayfish tails and cream and simmer for just 1 minute, until the crayfish have heated through. Add the basil and adjust the seasoning if necessary.

4 Drain the pasta and add to the pan. Toss together well, divide between 2 warmed pasta plates and serve immediately.

I used to frown on such flavour-smothering dishes as this cheese-and mustard-flavoured lobster thermidor, in spite of the fact that customers consistently ordered it over the years. But now I've mellowed, and made the dish far lighter than it ever was in the sixties, with only a thin film of well-reduced sauce and very little cheese. It's now incredibly popular in the restaurant once again.

lobster thermidor

SERVES 2

1 x 675 g (1¹/₂ lb) cooked lobster
25 g (1 oz) butter
2 large shallots, finely chopped
600 ml (1 pint) *Fish stock* (see page 200)
50 ml (2 fl oz) dry white vermouth, such as Noilly Prat
85 ml (3 fl oz) double cream
¹/₂ teaspoon English mustard
1 teaspoon chopped mixed *fines herbes* (chervil, tarragon, parsley and chives)
1 teaspoon lemon juice
15 g (¹/₂ oz) Parmesan cheese, freshly grated
Salt and freshly ground black pepper

1 To remove the meat from the lobster, twist off the claws and legs and discard the legs. Break the claws into pieces at the joints and crack the shells with a large knife. Remove the meat from each of the sections in as large pieces as possible. Now cut the lobster in half lengthways – first through the middle of the head between the eyes, then turn it around and cut it in half through the tail. Open it up and remove the tail meat from each half. Remove the dark intestinal tract from the tail meat and cut the meat into small, chunky pieces. Remove the soft, greenish tomalley and any red roe from the head section of the shell with a teaspoon and set it aside. Pull out the stomach sac (a slightly clear pouch) from the head section and discard. Transfer the cleaned half-shells to a baking sheet and evenly distribute the tail and claw meat between them with any red roe. Cover and set aside.

2 For the sauce, melt the butter in a small pan, add the shallots and cook gently for 3–4 minutes, until soft but not browned. Add the fish stock, vermouth and half the double cream and boil until reduced by three-quarters. Add the rest of the cream and simmer until the sauce has reduced to a good coating consistency. Whisk in the reserved tomalley, mustard, herbs and lemon juice, then season to taste with salt and pepper.

3 Preheat the grill to high. Carefully spoon the sauce over the lobster and sprinkle with the Parmesan cheese. Grill for 2–3 minutes, until golden and bubbling.

This is a crab soup that uses both the brown and white meat and has a reassuring sparseness of other ingredients: milk and cream, stock and a little rice to thicken it, plus a couple of mild flavourings – anchovy essence and mace. Crab – preferably one that has recently been boiled in sea water – seems to me to echo perfectly in a dish the sparse yet incredibly uplifting sea and mountain vistas of the highlands and islands of Scotland. I don't know why I'm suddenly thinking of this but I recall going into a little shop in a village miles from anywhere and, for some reason, deciding I needed some nail clippers. Not unnaturally, the shopkeeper said in the softest of burrs, that he didn't sell them. 'You could try biting them,' he said.

I should point out that the brown meat in crabs is not consistently good. You need one with a lot of light brown, creamy meat. Sometimes it is thin, dark brown, watery and rather bitter. However, even if it is good, don't use more than a quarter brown meat to white meat. Crabs should feel heavy for their size, so pick up one in each hand, of roughly the same size, and go for the heavier. If you can't find a crab with good brown meat, either leave it out or don't make the soup, but don't use frozen brown crab meat; it's awful. This soup is very rich so you will only need to serve small portions.

partan bree

SERVES 6–8

1 large cooked brown crab, weighing
about 1.5 kg (3 lb)
1.2 litres (2 pints) *Chicken stock*
(see page 200)
1 blade of mace
900 ml (1¹/₂ pints) full-cream milk
75 g (3 oz) long grain rice
150 ml (5 fl oz) double cream
A few drops of anchovy essence
Salt and freshly ground white pepper
A little cayenne pepper and a few
chopped chives, to garnish

1 Remove all the meat from the crab, reserving the pieces of shell. To do this, put the crab back-shell down on a board and break off the claws. Break off the legs, taking care to remove the knuckle joint where it joins the body. Lift up and break off the tail flap. Push the blade of a large knife between the body and the back shell and twist the blade to release it, then place your thumbs on either side of the body section and press firmly upwards until it comes away. Pull the feathery-looking gills (known as dead man's fingers) off the body and discard. Scoop out the brown meat from the centre of the body section with a teaspoon and keep it separate from the white meat. Cut the body section in half, using a large knife, and remove the white meat from all the little channels with a crab pick. Then crack the shell of the claws with the back of a knife and take out the meat, removing the thin piece of bone concealed within the meat of the pincer. Break the shell of the legs and hook out the white meat with the crab pick. Put the back shell on to a board with the eyes and mouth facing you and press on the little piece of shell located just behind the eyes until it snaps. Lift out and discard the mouth piece and stomach sac. Lastly, scoop out the brown meat from the back shell with a spoon and add it to that from the body. A crab of this size should yield about 275–350 g (10–12 oz) white meat and about 75 g (3 oz) brown meat.

2 Bring the chicken stock to the boil, add all the pieces of shell except the back shell, then add the mace blade and simmer for 15 minutes, turning the shells over now and then to extract as much flavour from them as possible.

3 Strain the stock through a muslin-lined sieve into a clean pan, add the milk, rice, half the white crab meat, 50–65 g (2–2½ oz) of the brown meat and any pink coral. Cover and simmer for 25 minutes, until the rice is really tender. Leave to cool slightly.

4 Liquidise the soup in batches until smooth, then return it to the pan and stir in the rest of the white crab meat, the cream and a little anchovy essence to taste. Reheat the soup without boiling and season with a little salt and some white pepper. Serve in warmed bowls, garnished with a sprinkling of cayenne pepper and a few chopped chives.

This is based on the memory of a dish from
Assaggi, a modern Italian restaurant above a pub in Notting Hill. It is
light, lively and perfectly composed for bringing the best out of fresh white crab meat.

crab with rocket, basil and lemon olive oil

SERVES 4

350 g (12 oz) fresh white crab meat
2 teaspoons lemon juice
4 teaspoons extra virgin olive oil,
flavoured with lemon if possible,
plus extra for drizzling
8 basil leaves, finely shredded
A handful of wild rocket leaves
Salt and freshly ground black pepper
Malden sea salt and cracked
black pepper, to garnish

1 Put the crab meat into a bowl and gently stir in the lemon juice,
olive oil, basil and some seasoning to taste.

2 Make a small, tall pile of the crab mixture on 4 plates, placing them
slightly off centre. Put a small pile of rocket leaves alongside. Drizzle
a little more olive oil over the rocket and around the outside edge of
the plate, sprinkle the oil with a little sea salt and cracked black pepper
and serve.

I got the idea of using Russian salad with seafood from Marco Pierre White's Belvedere restaurant in Holland Park. Before then, my last memory of making Russian salad was by the vat-load in the mid-sixties, in my lowly position as commis chef garde-manger in the Great Western Royal Hotel at Paddington Station. Faced with a Rumpelstiltskin task of turning endless carrots, beans and peas into neat little dice, I sometimes lost my enthusiasm. But the fact is that these freshly blanched vegetables, neatly cut and mixed with a good home-made mayonnaise, are a delight, and the perfect accompaniment to some good crab.

ramekin of crab with fresh russian salad and lamb's lettuce

SERVES 4

225 g (8 oz) fresh white crab meat
A small handful of lamb's lettuce
2 chestnut mushrooms, very thinly sliced
Salt and freshly ground black pepper

FOR THE RUSSIAN SALAD:
350 g (12 oz) waxy new potatoes, scraped clean
175 g (6 oz) carrots, peeled and halved
75 g (3 oz) fine green beans, topped and tailed
24 fine asparagus spears
50 g (2 oz) fresh peas
2 teaspoons lemon juice

FOR THE LEMON MAYONNAISE:
1 tablespoon lemon juice
Finely grated zest of 1 small lemon
1 teaspoon English mustard
1 egg
150 ml (5 fl oz) sunflower oil
150 ml (5 fl oz) olive oil

FOR THE HERB DRESSING:
2 tablespoons extra virgin olive oil
2 teaspoons white wine vinegar
2 teaspoons chopped chives

1 For the Russian salad, bring a pan of well-salted water to the boil (i. e. 1 teaspoon salt per 600 ml/1 pint water), add the potatoes and simmer until tender, then drain. Meanwhile, bring a second pan of well-salted water to the boil, add the carrots and cook until just tender. Remove with a slotted spoon and place in a bowl of cold water. Add the green beans to the pan and cook for 3 minutes. Remove from the pan and add to the bowl of cold water. Add the asparagus to the pan and cook for 2 minutes, then remove and place in the bowl of cold water. Finally, add the peas to the pan and cook for 1 minute, then drain and refresh in cold water.

2 Cut the potatoes into small dice (slightly less than 1 cm/½ inch). Cut the carrots and beans into similar-size pieces. Trim the top 5 cm (2 inches) from each asparagus spear and set aside. Cut the rest of the spears into similar-sized pieces to the other vegetables.

3 For the lemon mayonnaise, put the lemon juice, zest, mustard, egg and ½ teaspoon of salt into a liquidiser. Turn on the machine and gradually add the oils through the hole in the lid to make a thick emulsion. Put the vegetables into a bowl and gently stir in 4 tablespoons of the lemon mayonnaise and the lemon juice. Season well with salt and pepper.

4 Place a 9 cm (3½ inch) round cutter in the centre of each of 4 serving plates and spoon in some of the Russian salad. Lightly level the top, but don't press it down too hard, then carefully remove the cutter.

5 Line four 5.5 cm (2¼ inch) ramekins with cling film. Divide the crab meat between them and press down lightly, then invert on top of the Russian salad. Carefully remove the ramekins and clingfilm.

6 For the dressing, whisk the olive oil and vinegar with a little seasoning to taste and then whisk in the chopped chives. To serve, arrange 3 sprigs of lamb's lettuce, the asparagus tips and 3 slices of mushroom around the edge of each plate and drizzle around a little of the dressing.

The idea for this recipe comes from Alice Waters, of Chez Panisse in Berkeley, California. It appeals to me because baking the langoustines on salt subjects them to an intense dry heat, almost like a tandoor oven, which seems to accentuate their sweet flavour. The butter, melted with a lot of freshly cracked black pepper, is all that you need as an accompaniment. I used this recipe on the TV series to highlight the quality of the langoustines in Loch Torridon on the west coast of Scotland – a fishery recommended by the Marine Stewardship Council. Don't forget to put some finger-bowls or damp cloths on the table, as this is a dish for peeling the langoustines as you go along.

langoustines baked on rock salt with warm black pepper butter

SERVES 4

900 g (2 lb) large-crystal rock salt
100 g (4 oz) unsalted butter, softened
1 tablespoon cracked black peppercorns
1 tablespoon lemon juice
18 medium-sized, uncooked langoustines

1 Preheat the oven to 200°C/400°F/Gas Mark 6. Choose a very heavy pan with a well-fitting lid, large enough to hold all the langoustines in one layer. I have a 30 cm (12 inch) shallow Le Creuset casserole dish, called a buffet casserole, which is ideal.

2 Pour the salt into the casserole, spread out in an even layer and put the lid on. Heat it in the oven for 1 hour. Meanwhile, beat the butter with the cracked black peppercorns, put it into a small pan and set aside. Lay the langoustines on a tray and put them in the freezer for 30 minutes or so to kill them painlessly.

3 Remove the casserole from the oven and put the langoustines on top of the salt, nestling them down into it as you do so. Cover and bake for 6 minutes. Turn the langoustines over, cover the pan again and bake for another 2 minutes, until the langoustines are sizzling and cooked through. Meanwhile, put the butter over a low heat until it just melts. Stir in the lemon juice.

4 Pour about a tablespoon of the butter into the centre of each warm plate and put the langoustines on top.

This chowder evolved from a visit to Strangford Lough near Belfast. On the shores they grow herb celery, which is cultivated for its aromatic leaves rather than the fleshy stems. It is all too rare in Britain and yet it is good with fish. Chowders are immensely popular all over Ireland, so the marrying of the two, together with some langoustines and mussels from the lough, seemed highly appropriate. I've written the recipe using raw langoustines because the flavour is so much better, but they can be difficult to get. You could use good-quality frozen scampi (without breadcrumbs, of course) instead, if need be, because they are in fact the same thing. Simply add them to the soup 2–3 minutes before the end of cooking.

langoustine and mussel chowder with herb celery

SERVES 4

20 raw or cooked medium-sized langoustines
450 g (1 lb) mussels, cleaned (see page 74)
50 g (2 oz) butter
4 fresh bay leaves
50 ml (2 fl oz) dry white wine
1 small onion, chopped
50 g (2 oz) rindless dry-cured unsmoked bacon, cut across into short, fat strips
225 g (8 oz) potatoes, peeled and cut into small dice
1 tablespoon plain flour
300 ml (10 fl oz) full-cream milk
120 ml (4 fl oz) double cream
1 tablespoon chopped herb celery
2 water biscuits, crumbled
Salt and freshly ground black pepper

1 If using raw langoustines, put them into the freezer for 30 minutes to kill them painlessly. Then put them into a saucepan large enough to hold them and all the mussels and add 300 ml (10 fl oz) water and ½ teaspoon of salt. Cover, bring to the boil and steam for 3 minutes. Then uncover the pan and turn the langoustines over once or twice. Add the mussels, cover the pan again and steam for a further 3–4 minutes, until the mussels have all opened.

2 Tip the langoustines and mussels into a colander set over a large bowl, to collect all the cooking liquor. When they have cooled slightly, remove the langoustines and mussels from their shells and set aside. Alternatively, if using cooked langoustines, remove them from their shells and set aside. Put the mussels into a medium-sized pan with the water, then cover and cook over a high heat for 3–4 minutes. Drain, reserving the cooking juices as before, and remove the mussels from the shells.

3 Melt 25 g (1 oz) of the butter in a large pan, add the langoustine shells and 2 of the bay leaves and fry for 1 minute. Add the wine and the reserved cooking liquor and while it is bubbling away, crush the shells with the end of a rolling pin to release all their flavour into the liquid. Cook for 3–4 minutes and then pour back through the colander into the bowl.

4 Heat the rest of the butter in a pan, add the onion and bacon and cook gently until the onion is soft but not coloured. Add the diced potatoes and cook for 1–2 minutes. Stir in the flour, then add the milk, cream and bay leaves and strain in the flavoured cooking liquor through a fine sieve to remove any small pieces of shell. Simmer for 5–7 minutes, until the potatoes are tender.

5 Stir in the langoustines, mussels and herb celery and adjust the seasoning if necessary. Ladle into warmed soup plates and serve sprinkled with the crumbled water biscuits.

4 poultry

IN 1955 ELIZABETH DAVID WROTE, 'THE QUALITY OF POULTRY FOR THE TABLE HAS GREATLY IMPROVED DURING THE PAST YEAR OR TWO; THE REVOLT AGAINST BATTERY HENS IS HAVING ITS EFFECT.' BUT NEARLY 50 YEARS LATER WE'VE STILL GOT SOME WAY TO GO.

I CAN STILL REMEMBER THE TASTE OF THE FREE-RANGE CHICKEN I ROASTED FROM ROBIN READHEAD'S WONSTON ORGANIC POULTRY IN HAMPSHIRE. IT HAD A SLIGHT TOUGHNESS TO IT, NOT OFF-PUTTING, JUST A SIGN THAT THE BIRD HAD HAD PLENTY OF EXERCISE. AND WHEN ROASTED, THE SKIN HAD AN APPETISING BROWN CRISPNESS TO IT. NOT ONLY THAT, BUT THE GRAVY I MADE FROM THE ROASTING JUICES HAD MORE FLAVOUR. THIS IS THE SORT OF QUALITY OF POULTRY YOU NEED IN ORDER TO COOK THESE RECIPES.

Free-range Norfolk Black turkeys at Rookery Farm in Thuxton, Norwich.
Now a rare breed, Norfolk Black turkeys are renowned for their distinctive
gamey flavour.

Debbie, with whom I work on the recipes, found this French way of cooking chicken breasts, which is exactly what you want for *al fresco* living in the summer. You flatten the breasts out until they are quite thin and then cook them very quickly like you would a steak on a very hot, ridged griddle. We added a reduced red wine, red wine vinegar and shallot dressing and served it with watercress to give it a nice, minerally taste, resting the hot 'paillard' on top of the watercress briefly before serving to allow the flavours to mingle a little. It's a great example of the quick and easy food we all really love to cook.

grilled chicken paillard with watercress and a red wine dressing

SERVES 4

4 boneless free-range chicken breasts, weighing about 175 g (6 oz) each
120 ml (4 fl oz) red wine, such as Cabernet Sauvignon
1 teaspoon sugar
4 teaspoons red wine vinegar
4 tablespoons extra virgin olive oil, plus extra for brushing and to serve
1 shallot, finely chopped
25 g (1 oz) watercress leaves (large stalks removed), roughly chopped
Salt and freshly ground black pepper
Sautéed potatoes Lyonnaise (see page 195), to serve

1 Remove the skin from the chicken breasts. Put one breast skinned-side down on a large sheet of cling film and fold back the little loose fillet, which is now lying on top, to the outside edge of the breast. It will look a little like a heart. Cover with another sheet of cling film and flatten with a rolling pin or a cutlet bat to about 5 mm (¼ inch) thick – this is the 'paillard'. Repeat with the remaining chicken breasts.

2 Put the red wine, sugar and 3 teaspoons of the vinegar into a small, stainless steel pan, bring to the boil and simmer until reduced to 2 tablespoons. Pour into a small bowl and leave to cool, then stir in the olive oil, remaining vinegar, shallot and some salt and pepper to taste.

3 Heat a ridged cast-iron griddle or heavy-based frying pan until smoking hot. Brush the chicken breasts lightly with oil, season with salt and pepper and cook one or two at a time for 2 minutes on each side. Transfer to a plate and keep warm while you cook the rest.

4 Spoon the dressing into the centre of 4 warmed plates and scatter with the watercress leaves. Put the chicken paillards on top, cover each plate with another plate and leave for 5 minutes. Now uncover, drizzle a little extra virgin olive oil around the edge of the plate and serve with the sautéed potatoes.

POULTRY GRILLED CHICKEN PAILLARD

Coloradito means 'with a little red colour', and is one of the seven famous *mole* sauces of Oaxaca, in Mexico. I've shamelessly modified the recipe, since the original is extremely complicated, but from my memory of the chicken *mole* that I had at a restaurant called the El Naranja in Oaxaca, I would say that this is pretty close. It uses dried guajillo chillies, which have a sweet, refined heat and appear in a lot of classic Mexican salsas. They are available mail order from The Cool Chile Company (tel: 0870 902 1145).

chicken with coloradito

SERVES 4

900 ml (1¹/₂ pints) *Chicken stock* (see page 200)
8 chicken joints (thighs, drumsticks and/or part-boned breasts)
12 dried guajillo chillies
25 g (1 oz) sesame seeds
8 allspice berries
5 cm (2 inch) piece of cinnamon stick, broken into small pieces
1¹/₂ tablespoons dried oregano
85 ml (3 fl oz) sunflower oil
6 garlic cloves, sliced
1 onion, sliced
1 medium-thick slice of white bread, broken into pieces
1 slightly underripe banana, sliced
3 canned plum tomatoes
25 g (1 oz) plain or Mexican chocolate
Salt
Steamed rice (see page 198) or *Corn tortillas* (see page 124), to serve

1 Bring the chicken stock to the boil in a pan. Add the chicken joints and 1 teaspoon of salt, bring back to the boil and simmer for 10 minutes. Leave the chicken in the stock while you prepare the sauce.

2 Slit open the dried chillies and remove the stalks and seeds. Heat a heavy-based frying pan or cast-iron skillet and add the chillies. Using a wooden spatula, press them down into the hot pan until a small amount of smoke appears. Turn over and repeat on the other side. Transfer to a bowl and cover with 600 ml (1 pint) of hot water. Leave to soak for 15–20 minutes.

3 Add the sesame seeds, allspice berries and cinnamon stick to the hot frying pan and turn them for a minute or two until the sesame seeds are lightly toasted. Tip the mixture into a spice grinder, add the dried oregano and grind to a coarse powder.

4 Heat the sunflower oil in a large frying pan, add the garlic and onion and fry until beginning to brown. Add the bread and banana and continue to fry until the bread has taken on some colour. Transfer to a liquidiser and add the tomatoes, the drained soaked chillies, the dry ground ingredients from the spice grinder and another teaspoon of salt. Blend until smooth. Press through a sieve into a medium-sized pan to remove any large pieces of chilli skin, then bring to a simmer and cook for 5 minutes, stirring frequently.

5 Lift the chicken pieces out of the stock, remove the skin and add them to the sauce. Simmer for 10–15 minutes, or until the chicken is cooked through. Stir in the chocolate until it has melted and then serve with steamed rice or corn tortillas.

This recipe always evokes memories of wine trips to France. It's one of those old-fashioned dishes with lots of cream that you sometimes crave, particularly if accompanied by a really robust white wine such as a white Hermitage or even a Jura, whose sherry-like taste works with only a very few dishes but this is one of them. If you were to have such a wine, a splash of it to deglaze the pan adds a further subtle dimension, but it's the morels that really make the dish. I almost prefer the dried ones, which have a subtle smoky flavour that enhances many a sauce.

chicken fricassée with morels

SERVES 4

25 g (1 oz) dried morel mushrooms
1 x 1.5 kg (3 lb) chicken (or 2 chicken breasts and 4 thighs, skinned and boned)
The ingredients for the *Chicken stock* on page 200, minus the chicken (or 1.75 litres/3 pints chicken stock)
1 tablespoon sunflower oil
75 g (3 oz) butter
40 g (1½ oz) plain flour
1 large egg yolk
50 ml (2 fl oz) double cream
2 teaspoons lemon juice
Salt and freshly ground white pepper
Steamed rice (see page 198), to serve

1 Put the dried morels into a bowl and cover with 600 ml (1 pint) of hot water. Leave to soak for 40 minutes.

2 If you are using a whole chicken, cut off the legs and cut the breasts away from the bones. Skin the pieces and then bone the legs by making a cut along the length of each bone and cutting it away from the flesh. Make the chicken stock with the bones, following the instructions on page 200. Cut each breast lengthways, slightly on the diagonal, into 3 pieces and the leg and thigh meat into similar sized pieces.

3 Heat the sunflower oil and 15 g (½ oz) of the butter in a large, deep frying pan, add half the chicken pieces and cook over a medium-high heat for 8–10 minutes, until golden brown on both sides and just cooked through. Transfer to a plate, keep warm and repeat with the rest of the chicken, adding a little more butter to the pan if necessary.

4 Discard the fat left in the frying pan, add the chicken stock and leave to boil rapidly until reduced to 600 ml (1 pint).

5 Meanwhile, drain the morels and slice them. Melt 15 g (½ oz) of the remaining butter in another pan, add the morels and fry briefly for 1–2 minutes. Set aside with the chicken.

6 Strain the reduced chicken stock into a jug. Melt the remaining butter in a medium-sized saucepan, stir in the flour and cook gently for 1 minute. Gradually add the stock and bring to the boil, stirring. Add the morels and leave to simmer gently for 10 minutes.

7 Mix the egg yolk with the cream and stir in a large spoonful of the hot sauce. Stir the mixture back into the pan and cook very gently, without boiling, for 1–2 minutes, until slightly thickened. Stir in the lemon juice, some salt and pepper to taste, the chicken and the morels and reheat gently for a few minutes. Serve with steamed rice.

It's hard to think of a dish that makes British people more enthusiastic than a warm roast chicken and lots of salad, straight from the garden, served with new potatoes cooked with mint and tossed with a little butter. I'm particularly partial to the flavour of tarragon with chicken, and have roasted my chicken with it and made a mayonnaise-based tarragon dressing to go with the salad.

warm roast chicken salad with a creamy tarragon dressing

SERVES 4

50 g (2 oz) butter, softened
1 tablespoon roughly chopped tarragon
2 large garlic cloves, crushed
1 x 1.75 kg (4 lb) free-range chicken
1 tablespoon sunflower oil
Salt and freshly ground black pepper
Plain boiled new potatoes (see page 194),
tossed with butter, to serve

FOR THE DRESSING:
150 ml (5 fl oz) *Mayonnaise*
(see page 201), made with tarragon
vinegar and no mustard
1 teaspoon chopped tarragon
3 tablespoons single cream
1/2 teaspoon English mustard
1 teaspoon tarragon vinegar

FOR THE SALAD:
2 soft 'hothouse' lettuces,
leaves separated
4 vine-ripened tomatoes,
cut into wedges
1/2 cucumber, peeled and sliced
12 radishes, trimmed and halved
12 spring onions, trimmed and halved
4 large eggs

1 Preheat the oven to 200°C/400°F/Gas Mark 6. Mix together the butter, tarragon, garlic and some salt and pepper. Put the flavoured butter into the cavity of the chicken, then brush the outside of the bird with the oil and season with salt and pepper. Put into a small roasting tin and roast for 1¼ hours, basting the chicken with the buttery juices for the last 10 minutes of cooking.

2 Meanwhile, prepare the salad. For the dressing, whisk all the ingredients together until smooth and then season to taste. Arrange the lettuce leaves over a large serving platter with the tomatoes, cucumber, radishes and spring onions. Cover and leave somewhere cool.

3 Remove the chicken from the oven and leave to rest for about 15 minutes. Meanwhile, add the eggs to a pan of simmering water and boil for 8 minutes. Remove and set aside.

4 To joint the chicken, cut the breast meat away from the bones in 2 whole pieces and then slice each piece in half on the diagonal. Cut off the legs and cut them in half at the joint. Shell the warm eggs and cut them into quarters.

5 Arrange the warm chicken pieces and eggs over the salad and drizzle with a little of the dressing. Take to the table with a bowl of the remaining dressing and serve with buttered new potatoes.

I like smoked chicken breasts, especially those produced by the Cornish Smoked Fish Company of Charlestown in St Austell. But what I really love is fresh chicken that I've lightly smoked myself. In the seventies and eighties, the era of DIY, cookery books came out with instructions on how to build your own smoker, fill your own sausages, make authentic French baguettes and ferment your own redcurrant wine, and we all know how successful the latter was. Fierce hangovers, dry and fruitless wine that tasted of nothing but yeast. These days we are more practical, but actually a light smoking in a wok with some hardwood sawdust or chips is pretty easy to accomplish, and the sambal to serve with it is a blinder. Hardwood sawdust is available from DIY and garden centres.

home-smoked chicken breast with carrot, ginger and chilli sambal

SERVES 4

4 boneless chicken breasts, skin on
Hardwood sawdust, for smoking
Oil, for brushing
Salt and freshly ground black pepper
Coriander sprigs, to garnish
Sautéed potatoes (see page 195) and
Light green salad (see page 197),
to serve

FOR THE LIGHT BRINE:
50 g (2 oz) salt
600 ml (1 pint) cold water

FOR THE CARROT AND GINGER SAMBAL:
1 large carrot, sliced and then very
finely chopped
2 tomatoes, quartered, seeded and
finely chopped
2.5 cm (1 inch) piece of fresh ginger,
peeled and finely chopped
2 garlic cloves, finely chopped
1 medium-hot red Dutch chilli, seeded
and finely chopped
2 teaspoons dark soy sauce
1 teaspoon clear honey
2 teaspoons sunflower oil
1 tablespoon lemon juice
2 teaspoons sambal oelek (Indonesian
red chilli paste), or minced red chilli
from a jar
A small handful of mint leaves, chopped
A handful of coriander leaves, chopped
1/2 teaspoon salt

1 Make the brine by dissolving the salt in the cold water. Pour it into a shallow dish, add the chicken breasts and leave for 30 minutes, turning once. Remove them and dry on kitchen paper.

2 To smoke the chicken breasts, put a 2.5 cm (1 inch) layer of hardwood sawdust into a wok or deep frying pan and put it over a high heat until it begins to smoke. Then reduce the heat to low. Put the chicken on a lightly oiled cake rack, rest it on top of the pan and cover with a lid. Smoke the chicken for 5 minutes, then remove from the pan and set aside.

3 To cook the chicken, heat a ridged cast-iron griddle over a medium heat. Brush the chicken with oil, season with salt and pepper and put, skin-side down, on to the griddle. Cook for about 6 minutes, until the skin is richly golden, then turn over and cook for a further 6–7 minutes.

4 Meanwhile, mix together all the ingredients for the sambal.

5 Cut the chicken breasts on the diagonal into chunky slices. Place on warmed plates and spoon some of the sambal on top. Garnish with a sprig of coriander and serve with the sautéed potatoes and green salad.

Debbie Major, without whom these cookery books wouldn't happen on account of how I'm an idle dreamer, found this recipe in a book that I've long cherished but failed to notice myself, written by Richard Olney. It's a homage to a food hero of both his and mine, and to a way of life in Provence to which most of us aspire without the likes of Peter Mayle. Richard Olney was one of the best cookery writers of his time and in his book, *Lulu's Provençal Table* (Ten Speed Press, 2002), he captured the intellectual rigour combined with simple practicality of the best French family cooking.

I suppose I passed by this dish because of the importance of ginger in it but, as Debbie pointed out, you don't really notice it's there in the end. There is just an elusive niceness about the chicken, which is then served with some pasta quickly tossed with the roasting juices, sautéed tomatoes and fresh basil.

lulu's roast chicken with ginger, pasta, tomatoes and the roasting juices

SERVES 4

450 g (1 lb) vine-ripened tomatoes
1 x 1.5 kg (3 lb) free-range chicken
1 tablespoon finely grated fresh ginger
3 tablespoons olive oil
Juice of 1 lemon
50 ml (2 fl oz) dry white wine
350 g (12 oz) penne or small, tubular-shaped pasta
2 garlic cloves, crushed, then chopped
A large handful of basil leaves, finely shredded
Salt and freshly ground black pepper
Light green salad (see page 197), to serve

1 Preheat the oven to 230°C/450°F/Gas Mark 8. Skin, seed and coarsely chop the tomatoes. Toss them in a colander with ½ teaspoon of salt and set aside for 1 hour.

2 Season the chicken's cavity with salt and pepper, then smear the inside with the grated ginger. Put the bird into a roasting tin, rub all over with a little of the olive oil and season with some salt and pepper.

3 Roast the chicken for 20 minutes, then lower the oven temperature to 180°C/350°F/Gas Mark 4. Pour the excess fat from the roasting tin and pour a little lemon juice over the bird. Return to the oven and roast for a further 45 minutes, basting now and then with the rest of the lemon juice and then the white wine, until the juices from the thigh run clear when pierced with a skewer.

4 About 15 minutes before the chicken is ready, cook the pasta in plenty of well-salted boiling water (1 teaspoon salt per 600 ml/1 pint water) for about 12 minutes, until *al dente*.

5 Meanwhile, put the rest of the olive oil and the garlic into a large frying pan and place it over a high heat. As soon as the garlic starts to sizzle, add the tomatoes and toss over a high heat until a lot of the excess juice has evaporated and they give off a nice, slightly caramelised smell. Add the basil, toss again and remove from the heat.

6 Drain the pasta well. Remove the chicken from the oven, lift it on to a board and pour away any excess fat from the tin if necessary. Now tip any juices from the cavity of the chicken back into the roasting tin. Add the tomatoes, cooked pasta and a little black pepper to the roasting tin and turn everything together well in order to release all the roasting juices from the base of the tin.

7 Carve the chicken and divide between 4 warm serving plates. Spoon some of the pasta alongside and serve with the salad.

Much as I like chicken liver parfait or pâté, I think there are more things you can do with chicken (or duck) livers. This is quite special for me because it turns out much like my Mum used to make risotto in the sixties, when no one could get hold of Arborio or Carnaroli risotto rice. It just shows how food is really about what you get used to, because although I make perfect risotto for my sons, it was their grandmother's version, which she was still making in the nineties, that they liked best.

chicken liver and thyme pilaf with parmesan cheese

SERVES 4

50 g (2 oz) butter
1 onion, finely chopped
The leaves from 4 large sprigs of thyme
100 g (4 oz) chestnut mushrooms, thinly sliced
350 g (12 oz) long grain rice
750 ml (1¼ pints) *Chicken stock* (see page 200)
225 g (8 oz) chicken livers, cut into 2 cm (³/4 inch) pieces
4 garlic cloves, finely chopped
2 tablespoons chopped curly parsley
Salt and freshly ground black pepper
Freshly grated Parmesan cheese, to serve

1 Melt half the butter in a 20 cm (8 inch) heavy-based saucepan, add the onion and fry for 5 minutes, until soft and lightly golden. Add the thyme leaves and mushrooms and continue to cook for 2–3 minutes, until the excess moisture has evaporated from the mushrooms.

2 Stir in the rice and fry briefly until the grains are well coated in the butter. Add the chicken stock and ½ teaspoon of salt and bring quickly to the boil. Stir once, cover with a tight-fitting lid, then reduce the heat to low and leave to cook undisturbed for 15 minutes.

3 About 5 minutes before the pilaf is done, melt the remaining butter in a large frying pan. Add the chicken livers, garlic and some salt and pepper and cook over a high heat for 3 minutes, turning the livers now and then, until they are nicely browned on the outside but still pink and juicy in the centre.

4 Uncover the rice and gently fork through the chicken livers and the parsley. Serve sprinkled with finely grated Parmesan cheese.

The head of the cookery school, Paul Sellars, and I dreamt up this dish ages ago. I mean in the eighties, when duck only came in seriously undercooked, thinly sliced fans, with salads that were often dressed with raspberry vinegar and quite often raspberries too! We were being very subversive; we wanted something gutsy and immediate. We cooked the chicory until it was sweet and soft and aggressively cut the duck breasts into crosswise chunky pieces, not lengthways into thin slices. We made the sauce with manzanilla sherry and beef stock and finished it off with lots of ruggedly chopped parsley and it worked a treat. We were like a couple of punk rockers, breaking all the rules.

braised duck with chicory, parsley and manzanilla

SERVES 4

10 heads of chicory, weighing about 550 g (1¼ lb) in total
4 x 150–175 g (5–6 oz) duck breasts
40 g (1½ oz) butter
3 tablespoons dry sherry, such as manzanilla
1 tablespoon balsamic vinegar
300 ml (10 fl oz) *Beef broth* (see page 200)
2 teaspoons lemon juice
A handful of flat-leaf parsley leaves, roughly chopped
Salt and freshly ground black pepper
Mashed potatoes (see page 194), to serve

1 Cut each head of chicory lengthways into 4 or 6 wedges not quite through the root, so that the leaves stay together in one piece. Set to one side.

2 Season the duck breasts on both sides with salt and pepper. Brush the base of a large, heavy-based frying pan with a little of the butter. Put the pan over a medium-high heat and when hot, add the duck breasts, skin-side down. Cook gently for 6 minutes, until nicely browned, then turn them over and cook for a further 5 minutes. This should cook the breasts so that they are still slightly pink in the centre. Remove them from the pan, cover with foil and keep warm.

3 Pour away all but a couple of tablespoons of the duck fat left in the pan. Add the sherry and balsamic vinegar, bring to the boil and let them bubble away to almost nothing.

4 Add a little more butter to the pan, then add the chicory and sauté for 2–3 minutes, until lightly browned. Add the beef stock, ½ teaspoon of salt and 20 turns of the black peppermill. Bring to the boil and boil rapidly until the chicory is quite tender and the stock has reduced by about three-quarters.

5 Add the lemon juice and the remaining butter to the pan and boil to amalgamate, then finally sprinkle with the parsley.

6 Slice the duck breasts on the diagonal and put them on to 4 warmed plates, preferably deep bistro-style ones. Spoon the chicory on top and turn everything together briefly. Serve with mashed potatoes.

I think guinea fowl has a particularly satisfying flavour. It's probably as far into game as many people want to go and I think it's very successful in this dish, which has the idea of cassoulet as its theme.

baked guinea fowl with garlic beans and smoked sausage

SERVES 4

225 g (8 oz) dried haricot beans,
soaked in cold water overnight
1 tablespoon olive oil
1 x 1.5 kg (3 lb) guinea fowl
2 heads of garlic, broken into individual
cloves and peeled
25 g (1 oz) butter
50 g (2 oz) smoked bacon lardons
(short, fat strips)
The leaves from a large sprig
of rosemary
1 x 225 g (8 oz) smoked sausage,
cut into chunky slices
150 ml (5 fl oz) *Chicken Stock*
(see page 200)
Salt and freshly ground black pepper

1 Drain the beans, put them into a saucepan and cover with plenty of fresh cold water. Bring to the boil and simmer gently for 30 minutes– 1 hour (this will depend on the age of your beans), until just tender, adding 1 teaspoon of salt 5 minutes before the end of cooking. Drain and set aside.

2 Preheat the oven to 200°C/400°F/Gas Mark 6. Heat the olive oil in a medium-sized flameproof casserole. Season the guinea fowl, add it to the casserole and brown it on all sides. Turn the bird breast-side up and add the garlic cloves, butter, bacon lardons and rosemary to the casserole. Cover with a tight-fitting lid, transfer to the oven and cook for 30 minutes.

3 Add the beans, smoked sausage, chicken stock, ½ teaspoon of salt and some black pepper to the casserole and stir once or twice to coat everything in the cooking juices. Continue to cook, covered, for a further 30 minutes or until the guinea fowl is tender and cooked through.

4 To serve, lift the guinea fowl on to a board, cut off the legs and cut each one in half at the joint. Cut the breast meat away from the carcass in 2 whole pieces and slice on the diagonal. Divide the beans between 4 warmed, deep, bistro-style plates and place one piece of leg and some of the sliced breast meat on top.

5 meat and

NOWHERE IN THIS BOOK ARE THE RECIPES MORE
DIVERSE THAN IN THIS CHAPTER: BEEF RENDANG,
VIETNAMESE PHO, TOAD-IN-THE-HOLE, BEEF
CARPACCIO, COARSE PORK-AND-HERB TERRINE,
OR A FRENCH DAUBE DE BOEUF PROVENÇALE, AS
WELL AS A RECIPE FOR THE PERFECT CRACKLING
ON ROAST PORK. THE REASON IS, AS I'VE ALWAYS
SAID, *FOOD HEROES* IS ABOUT BRITISH AND IRISH
PRODUCE, IT'S NOT ABOUT TRADITIONAL BRITISH
COOKERY (THOUGH THE RECIPES FOR BEEF,
GUINNESS AND OYSTER PIE AND IRISH CORNED BEEF
WITH CABBAGE ARE JUST THAT). THESE ARE ALL THE
DISHES I LOVE TO EAT. FOOD WITH CHARACTER THAT
APPEALS TO OUR SENSE OF GOOD HUMOUR AND
LOVE OF INFORMAL PLEASURES.

offal

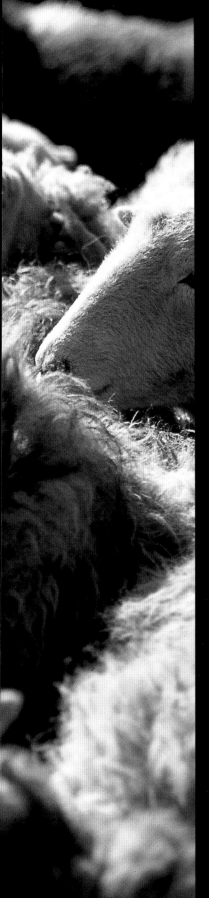

Herdwick lambs at Andrew
Sharp's farm in Dalton-in-
Furness, Cumbria.

The original recipe for beef carpaccio came from Harry's Bar in Venice, and was thinly sliced top rump of beef served ice-cold with a mustard mayonnaise-based dressing thinned down with lemon juice, milk and Worcestershire sauce. This was drizzled back and forth across the red beef in Jackson Pollock fashion. Indeed, the dish is so distinctive in appearance that it's become a bit of a sixties icon. Time has moved on, however, and now you're more likely to find carpaccio served with a sprinkling of good extra virgin olive oil, rocket and shaved Parmesan cheese. I like both methods but these days I prefer the cleaner taste of the rocket and Parmesan version. If you do want to make the Harry's Bar carpaccio, the dressing is on page 198 as part of the Lamb's lettuce, radicchio and green chicory salad.

beef carpaccio

SERVES 6

675 g (1½ lb) top rump of beef,
chilled overnight
Extra virgin olive oil
50 g (2 oz) wild rocket
25 g (1 oz) Parmesan shavings
Maldon sea salt flakes and freshly
ground black pepper

1 Using a long, razor-sharp, thin-bladed carving knife, cut the beef across into the thinnest possible slices. Arrange the slices over 6 chilled 25 cm (10 inch) plates, so that they cover the entire base with the edges of the slices just butting up together, but not overlapping very much.

2 Season the beef with some salt and pepper and then drizzle over a little olive oil. Pile the rocket leaves into the centre, scatter over the Parmesan shavings and serve straight away.

I am sure I'm not alone in returning from trips to country regions of France ecstatic with memories of steaks that were like nothing I'd tasted before. They would normally be called something like onglet or bavette, but back home you would generally draw a blank look from even the most skilled British butcher if you asked for a similar cut. The fact is that apart from the 'Sauvignon' and 'Chardonnay' of the steak world – sirloin and rump – we don't use many other cuts that you can simply grill and serve with crisp, thin chips and maybe a green or tomato salad. And while I'm getting enthusiastic about it, a couple of glasses of those fresh red wines that the French do so well, like Bourgeuil, Chinon, a cool Pinot Noir from Sancerre, or even a boozy rouge from Champagne. Debbie Major, with whom I write these books, has a brother-in-law called David, who is a real old-fashioned butcher in the village of Sway in the New Forest. He mentioned the muscle that runs along the blade bone in beef, which is normally sold as blade steak and used for braising. But here's the exciting bit. At the thinner end of the blade there's a short piece, about 15–20 cm (6–8 inches) long, known as the 'feather'. It's so called because of the arrangement of the muscles, which when cut into thin steaks have the shape and markings of a feather, but possibly also because of its extreme tenderness. Amazing when you think it costs a fifth of the price of fillet steak. If you buy the feather and have it sliced into steaks 5 mm (¼ inch) thick, then cook it quickly on a smoking-hot ridged iron griddle and serve 2 or 3 slices per person with anchovy butter, sprinkled with a little lemon juice, sea salt and freshly ground black pepper, some frîtes and a salad, you will have hit that memory of the steak with red wine in France, and you will be back there overlooking the Loire with your glass of Cabernet Franc. You won't get feather steak in a supermarket but any good butcher will know what you're talking about and will probably decide that you are a customer to be looked after in the future.

grilled feather steak with anchovy butter and frîtes

SERVES 2

The 350 g (12 oz) 'feather' end of a blade of beef, cut into slices 5 mm (¼ inch) thick
A little oil for cooking
Salt and freshly ground black pepper
Lemon wedges and *Thin chips* (see page 194), to serve

FOR THE ANCHOVY BUTTER:
2 salted anchovy fillets, rinsed of excess salt
25 g (1 oz) softened unsalted butter

FOR THE SALAD:
100 g (4 oz) lamb's lettuce
100 g (4 oz) frisée (curly endive)
1 cooked beetroot, peeled, sliced and cut into fine strips
2 tablespoons sunflower oil
1 tablespoon white wine vinegar
½ small garlic clove, crushed

1 For the anchovy butter, mash the anchovy fillets in a mortar with a pestle or in a small bowl with a fork until smooth. Add the butter and beat together until well mixed. Season with a little freshly ground black pepper.

2 For the salad, mix together the lamb's lettuce and frisée and place to one side of 4 large plates, then sprinkle over the beetroot. Whisk together the oil, vinegar, garlic, ½ teaspoon of salt and some freshly ground black pepper. Drizzle this dressing over the salad.

3 Brush the steaks on both sides with a little oil and season lightly with salt and pepper – don't forget that the anchovy butter will be quite salty. Heat a ridged cast-iron griddle over a high heat until smoking hot. Add the steaks (in batches if necessary) and cook for no more than 30 seconds on either side. Put alongside the salad, drop a little of the anchovy butter on top of each slice and serve straight away.

I have a considerable affection for this dish, as I learnt to cook it this way a long time ago in the sixties, when I was a trainee chef at the Great Western Royal Hotel at Paddington Station. The thing that impressed me was the speed with which you could turn it out and the practicality of the dish, which uses the tail end of the fillet. These were too thin for the tournedos that were the main use of beef fillet in that traditional, but actually very well run, kitchen. The dish has been completely ruined by

additions since those days but the original was lovely. We used to serve it with rice but I've since discovered that Jane Grigson, in her book *The Mushroom Feast* (Penguin Books, 1975), mentions that the Russians serve it with deep-fried matchstick potatoes called *kartoplia solimkoi*. For success with matchstick potatoes, you need Maris Pipers, and they must be starchy ones and not have been mishandled, as this causes the starch to turn into sugar. It's best to test a potato first, because the dish can be ruined by overly brown soggy chips. I've been known to buy Maris Pipers in two or three supermarkets until I've produced the blond, crisp chips I was after. This is my girlfriend Sarah's favourite dish, although she thinks it's better made with fresh cream rather than soured.

beef stroganoff

SERVES 4

675 g (1^1/$_2$ lb) beef fillet, preferably cut
from the tail end
65 g (2^1/$_2$ oz) unsalted butter
1^1/$_2$ tablespoons paprika (hot Hungarian,
if you like a little subtle heat)
1 large onion, very thinly sliced
350 g (12 oz) button mushrooms,
thinly sliced
3 tablespoons sunflower oil
300 ml (10 fl oz) soured cream
2 teaspoons lemon juice
A small handful of parsley leaves,
finely chopped
Salt and freshly ground black pepper

FOR THE MATCHSTICK POTATOES:
450 g (1 lb) floury potatoes, such as
Maris Piper, peeled
Sunflower oil for deep-frying

1 Cut the steak into slices 1 cm (½ inch) thick, then cut each slice across the grain into strips 1 cm (½ inch) wide. For the matchstick potatoes, cut the potatoes by hand into short sticks 3 mm (⅛ inch) thick, or use a mandolin. Set aside in a bowl of cold water. Heat some oil for deep-frying to 190°C/375°F.

2 Melt the butter in a large frying pan, add the paprika and onion and cook slowly until the onion is soft and sweet but not browned. Add the mushrooms and fry gently for 3 minutes. Transfer to a plate and keep warm.

3 Drain the matchstick potatoes and dry thoroughly in a clean tea towel or a salad spinner. Plunge into the hot oil and fry for 3 minutes, until crisp and golden. Drain briefly on kitchen paper and keep hot in a low oven.

4 Heat half the oil in the pan until very hot, add half the fillet steak and fry quickly, seasoning and turning it as you do so, for just over 1 minute. Transfer to a plate and repeat with the rest of the steak.

5 Return the onion mixture to the pan and pour in the soured cream. Bring to the boil and simmer for a minute or so, until thickened, then return the steak to the pan and heat very gently for 1 minute; the beef should not be cooked any further. Stir in the lemon juice and parsley and serve with the matchstick potatoes.

This is the first dinner party dish I ever cooked. I must have been 21 at the time. We started the meal with North Atlantic prawns and aïoli, then came Elizabeth David's daube de boeuf – with more garlic in some mashed potatoes – and petits pois à l'étuvée, followed by raspberries and cream. The occasion: a party in the barn at the back of our house on Trevose Head; the dinner guests, I think about six in number. It was a great summer's evening in late July and I've never forgotten it. What I particularly remember is everyone's astonishment at how much garlic I had put in the aïoli – it was positively hot – and the aromatic subtlety of the daube that went so well with the mashed potatoes and peas. There seem to be as many interpretations of a daube as there are of a bouillabaisse but everyone agrees that it should be cooked incredibly slowly (the French use the word *mijouter*, for which we have no translation but the closest would be 'at a tremble') in as tall and narrow a pot as possible. This allows a lot of meat to be cooked in a small amount of liquid, and that liquid to contain a lot of wine. The final daube, though deeply coloured, is remarkably fresh tasting and aromatic. If you can, leave it overnight, then the following day lift off the fat that will have set on the surface. Reheat the stew gently until hot and bubbling and you will find that the flavour will have improved even more.

la daube de boeuf provençale

SERVES 6

15 g (¹/₂ oz) dried porcini mushrooms
15 g (¹/₂ oz) butter
1 tablespoon olive oil
900 g (2 lb) blade steak (also known as
Jew's fillet), cut into slices
2 cm (³/₄ inch) thick
175 g (6 oz) bacon lardons (short, fat strips)
1 large onion, sliced
4 garlic cloves, sliced
2 carrots, sliced on the diagonal
1 fennel bulb, trimmed and cut into thin wedges
2 beef tomatoes, thickly sliced
Pared zest of ¹/₂ small orange
450 ml (15 fl oz) Cabernet Sauvignon wine
A bouquet garni of 2 thyme sprigs, 2 bay
leaves and a small bunch of parsley
Salt and freshly ground black pepper
Mashed potatoes (page 194) and the *Light green
salad* (page 197), to serve

FOR THE PERSILLADE:
1 garlic clove, peeled
A good handful of parsley leaves
1 salted anchovy fillet, rinsed of excess salt
6 capers
2 pitted black olives

1 Cover the porcini mushrooms with 150 ml (5 fl oz) hot water and leave them to soak for 20 minutes. Preheat the oven to 140°C/275°F/Gas Mark 1.

2 Heat the butter and oil in a flameproof casserole. Brown the pieces of steak in batches, turning them over to achieve a uniform colour on all sides. A set of tongs is ideal for this and no kitchen should be without one. Remove the beef and set aside. Reduce the heat a little, add the bacon lardons and fry until lightly golden. Add the onion and fry until lightly browned.

3 Return the meat to the pan and add all the other ingredients – i.e. the garlic, carrots, fennel, tomatoes, orange zest, soaked porcini mushrooms and their liquor, the red wine, bouquet garni, 1 teaspoon of salt and some pepper. Cover, transfer to the oven and cook for 3½ hours.

4 While the daube is cooking, make the persillade by coarsely chopping together the garlic, parsley, anchovy, capers and olives. Remove the daube from the oven, skim off all the excess fat from the surface, then sprinkle with the persillade and take to the table. Serve with mashed potatoes and the green salad.

Funnily enough, I happened on the joys of meatballs and pasta not in Italy but just outside Charleston, in South Carolina. We stopped off at a diner for lunch and had great meatballs flavoured with lemon and Parmesan, and it turns out that they are much more of an Italian–American dish anyway.

Last year I found myself having to make polite conversation with the mother of a friend of mine in Sydney called Vincenzo Parelli. Wildly searching for something to talk about, I mentioned that I loved her meatballs and that was it: future conversation was no problem. That's how it is with Italians – would that we didn't have to talk about the weather in this country.

I think that bucatini is the best type of pasta to go with meatballs – it just has the right texture when you eat it. It's the one a bit like macaroni but much thinner and longer, more like spaghetti.

polpettine in tomato sauce with bucatini

SERVES 4

4–5 tablespoons olive oil
1 small onion, finely chopped
2 garlic cloves, finely chopped
50 ml (2 fl oz) dry white wine
300 ml (10 fl oz) passata (sieved tomatoes)
120 ml (4 fl oz) *Beef broth* (see page 200) or *Chicken stock* (see page 200)
2 bay leaves
450 g (1 lb) bucatini or spaghetti
A large handful of parsley leaves, coarsely chopped
Salt and freshly ground black pepper

FOR THE POLPETTINE:
450 g (1 lb) good-quality lean minced beef, such as Aberdeen Angus
2 garlic cloves, finely chopped
Finely grated zest of 1/2 small lemon
25 g (1 oz) fresh white breadcrumbs
4 tablespoons full-cream milk
1 medium egg, beaten
A handful of parsley leaves, finely chopped
1 tablespoon chopped oregano
25 g (1 oz) Parmesan cheese, freshly grated, plus extra to serve
10 gratings of fresh nutmeg
2 tablespoons plain flour

1 For the meatballs, put the minced beef, garlic, lemon zest, breadcrumbs, milk, egg, parsley, oregano, Parmesan cheese, nutmeg, 1 teaspoon of salt and some freshly ground black pepper into a bowl and mix together well. Shape into small balls about 2 cm (¾ inch) in diameter.

2 Coat the meatballs lightly in the flour and shake off the excess. Heat 3 tablespoons of the olive oil in a large, shallow pan over a fairly high heat, add the meatballs and lightly brown all over.

3 Lower the heat to medium, add a little more olive oil if necessary, followed by the onion and garlic and cook gently for 2–3 minutes, until the onion has softened but not browned. Add the white wine and leave to bubble for a couple of minutes, then add the passata, stock, bay leaves and some salt and pepper. Simmer for 15 minutes, turning the meatballs occasionally, until the sauce has reduced and thickened slightly. Remove and discard the bay leaves.

4 Meanwhile, bring a large pan of well-salted water to the boil (1 teaspoon salt per 600 ml/1 pint water). Add the pasta and cook until *al dente*.

5 Drain the pasta well and put it into a large warmed serving bowl. Add the meatballs, their sauce and the parsley and toss together. Sprinkle with grated Parmesan and serve.

This is one of those brilliant Asian dishes, that you can get for breakfast or indeed any time of day, which is packed full of amazing flavours but is incredibly low in calories. It's also a very satisfying dish in that it allows the use of unprepossessing parts of beef or pork that would normally just be used for making stock. In my case I've used shin of beef, which goes to make a first-class broth and is then thinly sliced and added to the finished soup with some fillet steak, dropped raw into the boiling broth at the last minute. This, together with all the bright, fresh flavours of spring onions, mint, coriander and lime juice, gives the dish a lovely zest as it is served.

vietnamese pho (aromatic beef broth with fillet steak, spring onions and rice noodles)

SERVES 6

175 g (6 oz) flat dried rice noodles

75 g (3 oz) fresh beansprouts

6 large spring onions, thinly sliced

A small handful of mint leaves

A small handful of coriander leaves

1 medium-hot red Dutch chilli, thinly sliced

2 limes, cut into wedges

275 g (10 oz) fillet steak, very thinly sliced

Salt

FOR THE BROTH:

The ingredients for the *Beef broth* on page 200

900 g (2 lb) beef marrow bones

6 cloves

1 teaspoon black peppercorns

2.5 cm (1 inch) piece of fresh ginger, sliced but not peeled

7.5 cm (3 inch) piece of cinnamon stick

3 star anise

5 green cardamom pods

2 tablespoons Thai fish sauce (*nam pla*), plus extra to serve

1 Follow the instructions on page 200 for making the beef broth, adding the bones, spices and fish sauce to the pan. Bring to the boil, then simmer for 3 hours, skimming any scum and fat from the surface every now and then.

2 Strain the broth into a clean pan, reserving 225 g (8 oz) of the shin of beef but discarding all the other flavouring ingredients. You should be left with about 1.75 litres (3 pints) of liquid. (If you wish, you can chill the broth overnight; this is the ideal way to get rid of excess fat from the surface, as you can simply lift it off before reheating. Alternatively, skim the top for the last time to remove as much of the fat as you can.) Thinly slice the reserved shin and return it to the pan with 1 teaspoon of salt.

3 Put the rice noodles into a large bowl and cover with lots of boiling water. Leave to soak for 15 minutes, then drain and divide between 6 warmed, deep bowls. Top with the beansprouts and spring onions.

4 Put the mint and coriander leaves, chilli, lime wedges and some fish sauce into separate small bowls and arrange them on one large or 6 dinner plates.

5 Bring the broth back to a vigorous simmer. Take a large soup ladle and fill it with some of the fillet steak slices. Dip the ladle into the boiling stock and leave for 5–10 seconds, until the beef has changed to pale pink, then pour into one of the bowls and top up with extra broth to cover the noodles. Repeat for each of the bowls. Serve immediately, with the plate of garnishes, which can be added to the soup as wished.

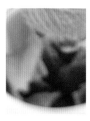

There is no other hot and aromatic beef stew like a rendang. It has a sweet and intensely spicy flavour and is unique in that the liquid ingredient, coconut milk, is cooked down to such an extent that it disappears with the spices into a pleasing sticky, brown coating for the beef, so that it becomes a truly 'dry' curry.

I find it much more satisfactory to make my own spice paste for this sort of dish, using whole spices. For this you will need either a very good mortar and pestle – there's a green granite one from Thailand, which is easy to get hold of here now and is by far the best – or a small electric grinder, where you grind the dry spices first and then mix them with the wet ones. There are also one or two liquidisers on the market now, notably the Breville, which has six blades, two pointing down, two horizontal, and two pointing up, which can grind wet and dry spices together in one go. These are in fact commonly available in India, too.

beef rendang with cucumber sambal

SERVES 4–6

A walnut-sized piece of tamarind pulp
1.5 kg (3 lb) blade or chuck steak,
cut into 2.5–4 cm (1–1¹/₂ inch) pieces
2 x 400 ml (14 fl oz) cans of
coconut milk
1 tablespoon light soft brown sugar
Salt
Steamed rice (see page 198), to serve

FOR THE SPICE PASTE:
1 tablespoon coriander seeds
1 teaspoon cumin seeds
2.5 cm (1 inch) piece of cinnamon stick
4 cloves
6 dried Kashmiri chillies, stalks removed
2.5 cm (1 inch) piece of fresh ginger,
peeled

1 Put the tamarind pulp into a small bowl with 85 ml (3 fl oz) warm water. Work the pulp into the water with your fingers until it has broken down and the seeds have been released. Strain the slightly syrupy liquid through a fine sieve into another bowl and discard the fibrous mixture left in the sieve.

2 For the spice paste, put the coriander seeds, cumin seeds, cinnamon, cloves and dried chillies into a spice grinder and grind to a fine powder. Put the ginger, garlic, chopped lemongrass, onion, turmeric and galangal, if using, in a food processor with the ground spices and 2 tablespoons of cold water and blend to a smooth paste.

3 Tip the paste into a large, heavy-based pan and add the reserved lemongrass layers, plus the beef, tamarind water, coconut milk, sugar and 1 teaspoon of salt. Bring to a simmer and cook, uncovered, for about 2½ hours, stirring now and then. Stir more frequently towards the end of cooking as the sauce becomes concentrated, to stop it sticking. Eventually the oil from the coconut milk will start to separate from the

6 garlic cloves, finely chopped
1 lemongrass stalk, outer layers
removed and reserved and the rest
roughly chopped
1 onion, roughly chopped
1 teaspoon turmeric
1 tablespoon chopped galangal
(optional)

FOR THE CUCUMBER SAMBAL:
1 cucumber
3 tablespoons coconut cream (from
a carton)
1 medium-hot red Dutch chilli, halved,
seeded and thinly sliced
1 medium-hot green Dutch chilli, halved,
seeded and thinly sliced
1 small red onion, very thinly sliced
2 tablespoons lime juice

sauce, but continue to cook for a minute or two longer to allow the meat and its coating to fry lightly in the oil. Remove and discard the lemongrass and adjust the seasoning if necessary.

4 For the cucumber sambal, peel the cucumber, cut it in half lengthways and scoop out the seeds with a teaspoon. Cut across into thin, half-moon-shaped slices and toss in a colander with 1 teaspoon of salt. Leave for 15 minutes, then rinse with cold water and dry on a tea towel. Mix with all the remaining sambal ingredients.

5 Serve the rendang with the cucumber sambal and some steamed rice.

When I first cooked this dark, full-flavoured pie in the restaurant during the mid-seventies, I have to confess I was a bit stingy with the oysters. We used to make it in individual brown earthenware dishes, and very popular it was too. Now that we can afford it, a lot more oysters go into it, which gives it a beguiling creaminess and also the same sort of salty, savoury taste that anchovies give to a French daube or oyster sauce to a Chinese beef stir-fry.

beef, guinness and oyster pie

SERVES 6

900 g (2 lb) braising steak, such as
blade or chuck, cut into 4–5 cm
(1½–2 inch) chunks
25 g (1 oz) plain flour
5 tablespoons sunflower oil
25 g (1 oz) unsalted butter
225 g (8 oz) small button mushrooms,
trimmed
2 onions, thinly sliced
½ teaspoon sugar
300 ml (10 fl oz) Guinness
300 ml (10 fl oz) *Beef broth*
(see page 200)
3 sprigs of thyme
2 bay leaves
2 tablespoons Worcestershire sauce
12 Pacific oysters
500 g (1 lb) chilled puff pastry
A little beaten egg, for brushing
Salt and freshly ground black pepper
Mashed potatoes (see page 194) and
Steamed sprouting broccoli (see page
196), to serve

1 Season the pieces of steak with salt and pepper, then toss with the flour and shake off but reserve the excess. Heat 3 tablespoons of the oil in a flameproof casserole or large saucepan and brown the meat in 2 batches until well coloured on all sides. Transfer to a plate.

2 Add another tablespoon of oil, half the butter and the mushrooms to the pan and fry briefly. Set aside with the beef. Add the rest of the oil and butter, the onions and sugar and fry over a medium-high heat for 20 minutes, until nicely browned. Stir in the reserved flour, then gradually add the Guinness and stock and bring to the boil, stirring.

3 Return the beef and mushrooms to the pan with the thyme, bay leaves, Worcestershire sauce, ¾ teaspoon of salt and some pepper, then cover and simmer for 1½ hours, until the meat is just tender.

4 Lift the meat, mushrooms and onions out of the liquid and put into a deep 1.2 litre (2 pint) pie dish. Rapidly boil the remaining liquid until reduced to 600 ml (1 pint). Remove and discard the bay leaves and thyme twigs, adjust the seasoning and pour into the pie dish. Stir everything together well and leave to cool.

5 Preheat the oven to 200°C/400°F/Gas Mark 6. To open the oysters, wrap one hand in a tea towel and hold an oyster in it with the flat shell uppermost. Push the point of an oyster knife into the hinge and wiggle the knife back and forth until the hinge breaks and you can slide the knife between the 2 shells. Twist the point of the knife upwards to lever up the top shell, cut through the ligament and lift off the top shell. Release the oyster from the shell, pick out any bits of shell and add them to the pie dish and push them well down into the sauce. Push a pie funnel into the centre of the mixture.

6 Roll out the pastry on a lightly floured surface until it is 2.5 cm (1 inch) larger than the top of the pie dish. Cut off a thin strip from around the edge, brush with beaten egg and press it on to the rim of the dish. Brush with more egg, cut a small cross into the centre of the pastry lid and lay it over the dish. Press the edges together well to seal. Trim away the excess pastry and crimp the edges to give it an attractive finish. Chill for 20 minutes.

7 Brush the top of the pie with beaten egg and bake for 30–35 minutes, until the pastry is crisp and golden and the filling is bubbling hot. Serve with the mashed potatoes and sprouting broccoli.

There is an avenue right in the middle of the Mercado de 20th Novembre in Oaxaca, Mexico that is wreathed in smoke right up to the vaulted corrugated iron roofs. There must be twenty charcoal grills creating an inferno of smoke. Each stall displays sheets of thin, lightly salted beef and they sell little pork sausages and escalopes of pork too, orange hued and rubbed with dried powdered chilli. At other stalls you buy the corn tortillas, guacamole, large spring onions, coriander and fresh salsa cruda (tomato salsa). You get the onions grilled along with the beef or pork, then you sit at long, white, formica tables with a pile of tortillas to make ever-varying combinations of the chewy but well-flavoured beef that tastes of the fire, the guacamole, onion and chilli. You rub shoulders with cheerful, reassuringly well-fed Mexicans and drink Corona or Victoria beer. This recipe is based on that whole experience. Masa harina (white maize flour) and tortilla presses are usually available by mail order from The Cool Chile Company, PO Box 5702, London W11 2GS (tel: 0870 902 1145), www.coolchile.co.uk.

tasajo con guacamole y salsa cruda (chargrilled beef tortillas)

SERVES 8

900 g (2 lb) rump of beef, very thinly sliced by your butcher (this should give you about 12 large slices)
Oil for brushing
15 large salad onions, halved length-ways or 30 spring onions, trimmed but left whole
2 limes, cut into wedges
Salt

FOR THE GUACAMOLE:
1 large, ripe avocado
1 jalapeño chilli (or other medium-hot green chilli), seeded and chopped
Juice of 1/2 lime
2 fat spring onions, chopped
1 small handful of coriander leaves, roughly chopped
2 tablespoons sunflower oil

FOR THE SALSA CRUDA:
350 g (12 oz) vine-ripened tomatoes, skinned
3 serrano chillies (or other medium-hot green chillies), roughly chopped
1 small onion, roughly chopped
A handful of coriander leaves

1 For the guacamole, peel and stone the avocado and put the flesh into a mortar or a food processor. Add the chilli, lime juice, spring onions, coriander, oil and 1/2 teaspoon of salt and mash or blend briefly, so it's still a little lumpy. Transfer to a serving bowl.

2 For the salsa cruda, put the tomatoes, chillies, onion and coriander into the cleaned bowl of the food processor and, using the pulse button, blend into a coarsely chopped sauce. Transfer to a serving bowl.

3 For the tortillas, put the masa harina, 1/4 teaspoon of salt and the water into a bowl and mix together to make a slightly moist dough. Shape the dough into about 36 balls. You need to line the tortilla press with a couple of 15 cm (6 inch) squares of cling film or baking parchment. You'll soon get the hang of pressing out the tortillas and peeling the liner away. Alternatively, roll them out by hand between 2 squares of cling film.

4 Place a dry, heavy-based frying pan over a high heat until very hot. Cook the tortillas in it, one at a time, for about a minute on each side, until lightly coloured with little brown spots. Wrap the tortillas in a tea towel and keep warm.

5 Lightly sprinkle each slice of beef (on both sides) with 1/4 teaspoon of salt and set aside for 10 minutes. Meanwhile, heat a ridged cast-iron griddle over a high heat until smoking hot. Brush very lightly with oil and cook the onions for 2–3 minutes, turning them once or twice, until tender. Transfer to a large warmed serving plate and keep warm.

6 Brush the griddle lightly with oil once more, add one of the beef slices and cook for 20 seconds on each side. Transfer to the serving plate with the onions and cook another 3 slices.

FOR THE CORN TORTILLAS:

675 g (1 lb 11 oz) masa harina

975 ml (33 fl oz) warm water

7 Garnish the plate of beef and onions with the lime wedges and take it to the table with the warm tortillas, guacamole and salsa cruda, so people can start eating while you cook the rest of the beef. The steak should be cut into pieces and used to fill the tortillas, flavouring it with the two sauces according to preference.

The evening after we filmed in The English Market in Cork, we ate a big plate of corned beef and cabbage in the café upstairs, and my gosh it was so good. That evening we checked into a large, family-run hotel in the city, looking forward to some more good local dishes, such as Irish stew with maybe some colcannon on the side. But we were only to discover that they had an 'adventurous' chef in residence, with such dishes as chargrilled kangaroo steak, crocodile tail and Atlantic shark with foie gras appearing on the menu. Seemed a bit of a shame.

In Ireland they call salted beef 'corned beef', so called because it is preserved with 'corns' (grains) of salt. On the British mainland we tend to call it salt beef, but they are essentially the same thing.

irish corned beef with cabbage

SERVES 4–6

2–2.25 kg (4¹/₂–5 lb) piece of corned beef (preferably the top rib, but silverside is good, too), see page 126 for suppliers

2 onions, peeled but left whole

6 cloves

2 bay leaves

8 black peppercorns

3 large carrots, peeled and each one cut into 3 pieces

4–6 evenly sized floury potatoes (about 100 g/4 oz each), peeled and halved

1 tightly packed, medium-sized green cabbage

Salt and freshly ground black pepper

Hot mustard, to serve (optional)

1 Rinse the beef under cold water to remove the brine and put it into a large but snugly fitting pan that is also large enough to hold all the vegetables. Stud the onions with the cloves and add them to the pan with the bay leaves, peppercorns and enough water to cover. Bring to the boil over a high heat, skimming off any scum as it rises to the surface. Then reduce the heat, cover and leave to simmer for 2–2½ hours, until the beef is tender, skimming the surface and topping up the water now and then if necessary.

2 Add the carrots and bring back to the boil. Then add the potatoes and simmer for 15 minutes. Meanwhile, wash the cabbage, cut it into 6 or 8 wedges and remove the thickest part of the core, but leave a little to help hold the leaves together. Add to the pan and simmer for 5 minutes, by which time all the vegetables should be tender.

3 Lift the beef on to a carving board and carve the meat across the grain into slices. Arrange the beef and vegetables on a large, warmed serving platter and moisten with a little of the stock. Serve with some hot mustard, if you wish.

MEAT AND OFFAL IRISH CORNED BEEF WITH CABBAGE

Every time I eat this dish I think of Gidleigh Park, the country house hotel just outside Chagford on the edge of Dartmoor. The proprietors, Paul and Kate Henderson, are another couple of food heroes of mine. The hotel is an American's idea of comfortable English life and generally it's a darn sight more comfortable than the average Englishman's view of English country life. I like the fact that this dish is on the breakfast menu as, after all, it is an American dish best served with a poached egg on top, and naturally a shake or two of Tabasco.

corned beef hash

SERVES 4

450 g (1 lb) cooked corned beef
(see page 125)
900 g (2 lb) floury potatoes, such as
Maris Piper, peeled and cut into
2.5 cm (1 inch) chunks
50 g (2 oz) butter
1 large onion, chopped
2 tablespoons white wine vinegar
4 large very fresh eggs
1 tablespoon Worcestershire sauce
A few shakes of Tabasco sauce
2 tablespoons chopped parsley
Salt and freshly ground black pepper

1 Shred the cooked corned beef using 2 forks. Put the potatoes in a large pan of boiling salted water and simmer for 5–6 minutes until just tender. Drain well.

2 Melt the butter in a large, non-stick frying pan, add the onion and fry gently for 4–5 minutes, until soft but not browned. Add the potatoes and continue to fry for 10–15 minutes, turning them now and then, until lightly browned.

3 Bring 5 cm (2 inches) of water to the boil in a wide, shallow pan. Add the vinegar and ½ teaspoon salt and reduce to a very gentle simmer. Break in the eggs and leave to poach gently for 3 minutes. Meanwhile, add the shredded corned beef to the frying pan, plus a little salt and some pepper. Continue to fry, turning the mixture over, for 2–3 minutes, until the beef has heated through. Then add the Worcestershire sauce and Tabasco and fry for another minute.

4 Spoon the corned beef hash onto 4 warmed plates. Remove the eggs with a slotted spoon, drain briefly on kitchen paper, and serve on top. Scatter over the parsley and serve with extra Tabasco or some chilli sauce, if you wish.

FOR CORNED BEEF BY MAIL ORDER:
James McGeogh, Lake Road, Oughterard, Galway, Ireland (tel: 00 353 91 552351)
James Whelan Butchers, Oakville Shopping Centre, Clonmel, Co. Tipperary, Ireland (tel: 00 353 52 22927), www.jameswhelan-butchers.com
M. Newitt & Sons, 10, High Street, Thame, Oxfordshire OX9 2BZ (tel: 01844 212103), www.newitt.co.uk

The reason oxtail tastes so luscious is due to the presence of a large amount of connective tissue, which allows the cattle to whisk their tails and zap flies so effectively. But there is also a great deal of fat, so it's essential to double-cook the casserole to extract the maximum. After the first long, slow simmer and an overnight spell in the fridge, most of the fat will have settled obligingly on the top in an easy-to-remove layer. This is one of Debbie's dishes and I think the addition of some plump prunes soaked in Cognac gives it a pleasingly exotic touch. I'm particularly partial to the crisp, buttery breadcrumbs that you scatter over the finished dish.

twice-cooked oxtail and prune casserole

SERVES 6

2 oxtails, weighing about 2 kg (4^1/$_2$ lb) in total, cut into 5 cm (2 inch) pieces
50 g (2 oz) plain flour, seasoned with salt and pepper
4 tablespoons sunflower oil
50 g (2 oz) butter
1 large onion, chopped
600 ml (1 pint) *Beef broth (see page 200)*
450 ml (15 fl oz) red wine
1 tablespoon redcurrant jelly
3 garlic cloves, sliced
A bouquet garni of parsley stalks, bay leaves and thyme
225 g (8 oz) dried Agen prunes
4 tablespoons Cognac
350 g (12 oz) button onions, peeled
2 celery stalks, sliced
350 g (12 oz) carrots, sliced
350 g (12 oz) leeks, sliced
25 g (1 oz) fresh white breadcrumbs
2 tablespoons chopped curly-leaf parsley
Salt and freshly ground black pepper
Mashed potatoes (see page 194), to serve

1 Trim any excess fat from the oxtail and then toss the pieces in the seasoned flour, shaking off and reserving any excess. Heat half the oil in a large, flameproof casserole, add the oxtail and fry in 2 batches, until well browned all over. Transfer to a plate and set aside.

2 Add another tablespoon of the oil and 25 g (1 oz) of the butter to the casserole, then add the onion and cook, stirring, for about 7 minutes, until nicely coloured. Stir in any reserved seasoned flour and cook for 1 minute.

3 Gradually stir in the beef broth, red wine and redcurrant jelly and bring to the boil. Return the oxtail to the casserole with the garlic and bouquet garni and season with ½ teaspoon of salt and plenty of black pepper. Cover and leave to simmer gently for 2½ hours, turning the oxtail pieces from time to time, until just tender, but not falling apart.

4 Remove from the heat and leave to cool, then chill overnight in the fridge. Put the prunes into a small bowl and pour over the brandy. Cover and leave to soak overnight.

5 The next day, heat the rest of the oil in a large saucepan, add the button onions and fry for 1 minute. Add 15 g (½ oz) of the remaining butter, then the celery, carrots and leeks, and fry for 3 minutes.

6 Lift the fat off the top of the oxtail casserole and discard. Gently reheat the casserole, then stir in the vegetables and prunes and simmer, uncovered, for 20–30 minutes until the vegetables are tender.

7 Heat the remaining 15 g (½ oz) butter in a frying pan, add the breadcrumbs and fry gently for 3–4 minutes, until lightly golden. Season and stir in the parsley. Sprinkle the breadcrumbs on top of the casserole and serve with lots of mashed potatoes.

I don't know if my recipe for osso buco is the same as Bertorelli's but it's one of those dishes I associate with a certain period of my life in London. I have particular memories of the finish to the dish – gremolata, that exciting mixture of finely chopped lemon zest, garlic and parsley. What I love about osso buco is getting it with the marrow still in the shinbones so that you can pick it out, that silky, unctuous texture adding an immeasurable pleasure to an already memorable dish. It's always served with risotto Milanese but I leave out the traditional extra beef marrow and Parmesan, which I would only include if this simple and perfect saffron-flavoured risotto was to be served on its own.

osso buco

SERVES 4

1.5 kg (3 lb) shin of veal, cut into slices
4 cm (1¹/₂ inches) thick
4 tablespoons olive oil
25 g (1 oz) plain flour
1 onion, finely chopped
1 small carrot, finely chopped
1 celery stalk, finely chopped
Leaves from 1 sprig of rosemary
2 sage leaves
150 ml (5 fl oz) dry white wine
2 tomatoes, skinned and chopped

1 Season the slices of shin with ½ teaspoon of salt and leave for 20 minutes before cooking. Heat the olive oil in a heavy-based flameproof casserole. Coat the pieces of shin economically with the flour, pat off the excess and fry until nicely browned on both sides. Transfer to a plate, taking care not to disturb the marrow.

2 Add the vegetables, rosemary leaves and sage to the pan and fry until lightly browned. Add the wine and tomatoes and cook until the wine has almost completely evaporated. Return the meat to the pan and add the beef stock, pared lemon zest, ½ teaspoon of salt and some pepper. Bring to the boil, then cover and simmer gently for

600 ml (1 pint) *Beef broth* (see page 200)

1 pared strip of lemon zest

Salt and freshly ground black pepper

FOR THE RISOTTO MILANESE:

1.2 litres (2 pints) *Beef broth*
(see page 200)

A small pinch of saffron strands

50 g (2 oz) unsalted butter

2 shallots, finely chopped

225 g (8 oz) risotto rice, such as
Carnaroli or Arborio

FOR THE GREMOLATA:

1 garlic clove, peeled

A small handful of flat-leaf parsley
leaves

1 pared strip of lemon zest

1 hour. Uncover and skim off the excess fat from the surface. Increase the heat slightly and simmer more vigorously for 30 minutes to reduce and concentrate the flavour of the sauce.

3 Meanwhile, make the risotto Milanese. Put the beef broth into a pan and bring to the boil. Reduce the heat, add the saffron and keep hot. Melt half the butter in a pan, add the shallots and cook gently for 3–4 minutes, until soft but not browned. Add the rice and turn it over for a couple of minutes until all the grains are coated in the butter. Add a ladleful of the hot stock and stir over a medium heat until it has all been absorbed before adding another. Continue like this for about 20 minutes, stirring constantly, until you have added all the stock and the rice is tender and creamy but still a little *al dente*. Stir in the remaining butter and season to taste with salt and pepper.

4 For the gremolata, chop the garlic, parsley and lemon together quite finely. Sprinkle it over the top of the stew and then spoon into 4 warmed, deep plates. Spoon the risotto Milanese alongside and serve.

I had forgotten how good Wiener Schnitzel was until I was presented with the very thing at a friend's house in Sydney quite recently. I think the secret of cooking for friends is to do something that doesn't appear to be a lot of trouble, the sort of food that everyone knows and loves. Wiener Schnitzel is just that. You can make them up some time ahead and keep them chilled in the fridge, then serve them up with a nice green salad and some thin chips. An agreeable chilled white wine, such as Adelaide Hills Sauvignon Blanc, would also go down a treat, and all would be right with the world.

You can buy prepared veal escalopes from your butcher, but should you want to do them yourself, they are cut from the topside or top rump. You start off with slices 1 cm (½ inch) thick, put them between 2 large sheets of cling film and beat out the meat with a rolling pin until it is about 5 mm (¼ inch) thick and about 23 cm (9 inches) across. This is what makes the dish so impressive. They have to be big – so often you find that the pieces of meat are too small or too thick.

wiener schnitzel

1 egg, beaten
1 tablespoon extra virgin olive oil
100 g (4 oz) fine white breadcrumbs,
made from dry, stale bread
15 g (¹/₂ oz) plain flour
2 x 175 g (6 oz) veal escalopes
Sunflower oil for shallow-frying
Salt and freshly ground black pepper
Thin chips (page 194) and *Light green
salad* (page 197), to serve

FOR THE GARNISH:
4 anchovy fillets in oil, drained
4 green olives stuffed with pimento
15 g (¹/₂ oz) butter
1 teaspoon nonpareilles capers, drained
and rinsed
A small handful of curly-leaf parsley
leaves, finely chopped
2 lemon wedges

1 For the garnish, wrap an anchovy fillet around each olive. Melt the butter in a small pan and keep warm. Set aside with the capers, chopped parsley and lemon wedges.

2 Beat the egg with the olive oil, a tablespoon of water, ½ teaspoon of salt and 20 turns of the black peppermill, then pour it into a large, shallow dish. Spread the breadcrumbs out in a large, shallow baking tray and the flour in another.

3 Dip one of the escalopes into the flour and pat off the excess. Then dip it into the beaten egg, lift it up and allow the excess to run off. Finally, dip it into the breadcrumbs, pressing them on well to give a good, even coating. Shake off any excess. Coat the second escalope in the same way.

4 Pour 1 cm (½ inch) sunflower oil into a large, deep frying pan and heat it to 190°C/375°F. Lower one of the escalopes into the hot oil, turn the heat down to medium and leave it to cook for 1 minute, until crisp and golden. Turn over and cook for a further minute. Transfer to a tray lined with kitchen paper and keep hot in a low oven while you cook the second escalope.

5 Put the escalopes on to 2 large, warmed plates and put the anchovy and olive rolls alongside. Pour over the hot melted butter, scatter with the capers and chopped parsley and serve with the lemon wedges, thin chips and the green salad.

The whole point of this dish is balance. I was looking for some interesting cuts of lamb, such as tender and lean loin and well-flavoured kidneys, to be set off by the tartness of some good tomatoes grilled with a bit of spice and a big pile of lovely mashed potato and cabbage – colcannon. All this is served with a roast-style gravy. This might seem like a lot of work but is no more effort than meat and two veg, and I think you'll find the whole thing hangs together rather well.

roast loin of lamb with kidneys, grilled devilled tomatoes and colcannon

SERVES 4

1 x 900 g (2 lb) boned and rolled loin of lamb, skin removed
4 lambs' kidneys, cut in half and the cores snipped out with scissors
150 ml (5 fl oz) *Chicken stock* (see page 200)
1 teaspoon plain flour
Salt and freshly ground black pepper

FOR THE COLCANNON:
675 g (1¹/₂ lb) peeled Maris Piper potatoes, cut into chunks
225 g (8 oz) curly kale or spring cabbage, thinly sliced
25 g (1 oz) butter
1 leek or small onion, chopped
150 ml (5 fl oz) full-cream milk
Freshly ground white pepper

FOR THE DEVILLED TOMATOES:
¹/₄ teaspoon cayenne pepper
1 teaspoon English mustard
¹/₂ teaspoon Worcestershire sauce
15 g (¹/₂ oz) softened butter
4 vine-ripened tomatoes, cut in half
Oil for brushing

1 Preheat the oven to 230°C/450°F/Gas Mark 8. For the colcannon, put the potatoes into a pan of water salted at the rate of 1 teaspoon per 600 ml (1 pint). Bring to the boil and simmer until tender. Meanwhile, season the lamb with salt and pepper, put it into a roasting tin and roast for 30 minutes. When it is done, remove from the oven and transfer to a board. Cover with foil and leave to rest for about 10 minutes.

2 While the lamb is cooking, put 1 cm (½ inch) water into a large pan and bring to the boil. Add ½ teaspoon of salt and the cabbage and cook over a vigorous heat for 4–5 minutes, until just tender (but not mush!). Drain the potatoes and leave the steam to die down. Drain the cabbage well. Melt the butter in the pan in which the cabbage was cooked, then add the leek or onion and cook gently for 7–8 minutes, until very soft but not coloured. Pass the potatoes through a potato ricer into the pan and add the cabbage, milk and white pepper to taste. Mix together well and keep hot.

3 Preheat the grill to high. For the devilled tomatoes, mix together the cayenne pepper, mustard, Worcestershire sauce, butter, ¼ teaspoon of salt and some black pepper in a small bowl. Put the tomatoes on an oiled baking tray or the rack of the grill pan, brush with a little oil and season lightly with salt and pepper. Grill for 3–4 minutes, until beginning to soften. Season the kidneys, add them to the tray and dot the tomatoes with some of the devilled butter. Grill for a further 4–5 minutes, until they are both cooked through.

4 Meanwhile, pour off any fat left in the roasting tin, place it over a medium-high heat and stir in the flour. Add the stock and boil rapidly for a minute or two until reduced to a well-flavoured gravy, scraping the base of the tin with a wooden spoon to release all the caramelised juices. Strain into a small pan, adjust the seasoning and keep warm.

5 Carve the lamb across into thin slices. Spoon the colcannon on to 4 warmed plates and place the slices of lamb alongside. Add the kidneys and devilled tomatoes, pour some gravy over the lamb and serve.

You might think this is quite an odd dish to have in a book largely about British food but it's become pretty much part of our own cooking now. Indeed, it brings back memories to me of a little Greek restaurant down the Cowley Road in Oxford, when I was an undergraduate in the early seventies, called the New Excelsior Café, which did pretty good moussaka, served, as I recall, with roast potatoes. We would usually go after the pub on a Sunday lunchtime and I would have been wearing any one of a sequence of six velvet jackets from Take Six in Carnaby Street, each of which lasted only about six weeks.

The bits that make all the difference, and transform the dish into something quite special, are exceptionally good minced lamb, a tomato sauce flavoured only with cinnamon and preferably Greek oregano, a smooth béchamel sauce with a little cheese, and a thick base of fried aubergines. It needs none of the other bits and bobs that seem to crop up regularly, like green peppers, chilli or raisins.

moussaka

SERVES 6

150–175 ml (5–6 fl oz) olive oil
1 large onion, finely chopped
3 garlic cloves, crushed
900 g (2 lb) lean minced lamb
50 ml (2 fl oz) white wine (a generous splash)
400 g (14 oz) can of chopped tomatoes
5 cm (2 inch) piece of cinnamon stick
A handful of fresh oregano leaves, preferably wild Greek oregano, chopped
3 large aubergines, cut lengthways into slices 5 mm (¹/₄ inch) thick
Salt and freshly ground black pepper

FOR THE TOPPING:
75 g (3 oz) butter
75 g (3 oz) plain flour
600 ml (1 pint) full-cream milk
50 g (2 oz) Parmesan cheese, freshly grated
2 medium eggs, beaten

1 Heat 2 tablespoons of the oil in a pan, add the onion and garlic and fry until just beginning to brown. Add the minced lamb and fry over a high heat for 3–4 minutes. Add the wine, tomatoes, cinnamon and oregano and simmer gently for 30–40 minutes while you prepare everything else.

2 Heat a frying pan until it is very hot, add 1 tablespoon of the oil and a layer of aubergine slices and fry quickly until tender and lightly coloured on both sides. Lift out with tongs and arrange over the base of a deep 2.5–2.75 litre (4½–5 pint) ovenproof baking dish. Season lightly with a little salt and pepper. Repeat with the rest of the oil and the aubergines, seasoning each layer as you go.

3 For the topping, melt the butter in a pan, add the flour and cook, stirring, over a medium heat for 1 minute. Gradually beat in the milk, then bring to the boil, stirring. Simmer very gently for 10 minutes, stirring occasionally. Add the cheese and some salt and pepper to taste. Cool slightly and then beat in the eggs.

4 Preheat the oven to 200°C/400°F/Gas Mark 6. Remove the cinnamon stick from the lamb sauce, season to taste with some salt and pepper and spread it over the aubergines. Pour the topping over the sauce and bake for 25–30 minutes, until golden and bubbling.

I fondly recall the curries my mother used to cook when we were little. We only ever had two, a wet one with currants, apple and a Sharwood's curry powder, and a much drier one made with minced lamb, which she would often make into a Raj-style shepherd's pie. It was delicious, and we always had sweet mango chutney with it. I later realised that the dish was very similar to a *kheema*, though that would have been made with fresh peas and served with steamed rice. You can indeed just add some peas to the spicy minced lamb sauce and serve it with steamed basmati rice.

shepherd's pie as cooked in india

SERVES 4

2 tablespoons sunflower oil

1 onion, finely chopped

4 garlic cloves, crushed

2.5 cm (1 inch) piece of fresh ginger, peeled and finely grated

900 g (2 lb) lean minced lamb

1 medium-hot red Dutch chilli, seeded and finely chopped

1 teaspoon turmeric

1 tablespoon ground coriander

1 tablespoon ground cumin

1 vine-ripened tomato, chopped

1 tablespoon tomato purée

1 teaspoon tamarind paste

300 ml (10 fl oz) *Chicken stock* (see page 200)

A handful of coriander leaves, chopped

Salt and freshly ground black pepper

FOR THE POTATO TOPPING:

1.25 kg (2½ lb) floury potatoes, such as Maris Piper or King Edward, peeled and cut into chunks

50 g (2 oz) butter

A little full-cream milk

1 Heat the oil in a pan, add the onion, garlic and ginger and fry until the onion is soft and just beginning to brown. Add the minced lamb, chilli, turmeric, coriander and cumin and fry until the meat is lightly browned.

2 Stir in the tomato, tomato purée, tamarind paste and stock, season with some salt and plenty of black pepper and simmer for 30 minutes, until the liquid has reduced and the mixture has thickened but is still nice and moist. Stir in the chopped coriander and transfer the mixture to a shallow 1.75 litre (3 pint) ovenproof dish.

3 Preheat the oven to 200°C/400°F/Gas Mark 6. Put the potatoes into a large pan of water salted at the rate of 1 teaspoon per 600 ml (1 pint). Bring to the boil and simmer until tender. Drain, leave until the steam has died down, then pass them through a potato ricer (or mash them). Return to the pan, beat in the butter and season with salt and pepper. Add enough milk to form a soft, spreadable mash.

4 Spoon the potato over the lamb mixture and mark the surface with a fork. Bake for 30–35 minutes, until piping hot and golden brown.

This recipe comes from Shaun Hill, who owns and cooks at the Merchant House in Ludlow, Shropshire. I think I was moved to mention that the whole town of Ludlow was a food hero of mine because it all works gastronomically, probably mostly because of Shaun. His and two or three other restaurants have created a 'definitely worth a detour' stop-off, and the food shops have grown, multiplied and got better and better. What I love about his restaurant is that he has no staff; he runs it with his wife, Anja. He cooks, using the most modest equipment, and builds his recipes entirely around the capacity of his kitchen. It takes a chef of considerable experience, which he is, to do that. Most chefs want ever more sophisticated stoves, grills and fryers. Shaun has disciplined himself to cook within those confines and turns out some of the most attractive food to be found anywhere, including this dish. When you try it, you'll know what I mean.

lambs' sweetbreads with olive potato cakes

SERVES 6 AS A STARTER

675 g (1¹/₂ lb) lambs' sweetbreads
1.75 litres (3 pints) water
1 tablespoon white wine vinegar
1 shallot, finely chopped
A little olive oil for brushing
Salt and freshly ground black pepper

FOR THE OLIVE POTATO CAKES:
550 g (1¹/₄ lb) peeled floury potatoes,
such as Maris Piper, cut into chunks
1 medium egg yolk
20 green olives stuffed with anchovies,
finely chopped
25 g (1 oz) plain flour
1 medium egg, beaten
100 g (4 oz) fresh white breadcrumbs
Sunflower oil for shallow-frying

FOR THE CAPER, SHALLOT AND
PARSLEY DRESSING:
1 egg yolk
1 tablespoon Dijon mustard
1 teaspoon white wine vinegar
120 ml (4 fl oz) olive oil
120 ml (4 fl oz) sunflower oil
120 ml (4 fl oz) *Chicken stock*
(see page 200) or water
1 tablespoon nonpareilles capers,
drained and rinsed
1 tablespoon finely chopped shallots
1 tablespoon chopped curly-leaf parsley

1 For the potato and olive cakes, put the potatoes into a large pan of water salted at the rate of 1 teaspoon per 600 ml (1 pint) and bring to the boil. Simmer until just tender, then drain well. When the steam has died down, pass them through a potato ricer (or mash them), return to the pan and stir in the egg yolk, olives and some seasoning to taste. Divide the mixture into 12 and shape them into patties. Cover and chill for 30 minutes or until needed.

2 Soak the sweetbreads in cold water for 1 hour. Drain and then trim away any membranes and unappetising-looking bits from the outside. Put them into a pan with the water, vinegar, shallot and some pepper, bring to the boil and simmer gently for 1 minute. Remove the pan from the heat and leave them to cool in the liquid.

3 For the dressing, whisk the egg yolk, mustard and vinegar together in a bowl. Gradually whisk in the oils to make a mayonnaise-like mixture.

4 To finish the potato and olive cakes, pour about 1 cm (½ inch) sunflower oil into a large frying pan and heat it to 180°C/350°F. Coat them in the flour, then in the egg and finally in the breadcrumbs and fry for 2 minutes on each side, until crisp and golden. Transfer to a baking tray and keep hot in a low oven.

5 Remove the sweetbreads from the cooking liquor and pat dry with kitchen paper. Slice the larger ones in half on the diagonal to get them as thin as possible. Brush them with olive oil and season with a little salt and pepper. Heat a heavy-based frying pan over a high heat until smoking hot, add about a third of the sweetbreads and sear for 1 minute on each side or until nicely caramelised. Transfer to a baking tray and keep hot while you cook the remainder.

6 To finish the dressing, bring the stock or water, capers and shallots to the boil in a small, shallow pan. Remove the pan from the heat and whisk in 6 tablespoons of the mustardy mayonnaise to make a sauce with the consistency of double cream. If it is not quite thick enough, stir over a low heat for a minute or two until thickened, but don't let it boil or it will curdle. Stir in the parsley and some seasoning to taste.

7 Spoon the dressing on to 4 warmed plates and put the sweetbreads on top. Put the potato and olive cakes alongside and serve.

The Mangal Ocakbasi is in Arcola Street in Dalston, North London. It's one of those places much loved by chefs – an ethnic restaurant that serves the locals and outsiders 'in the know', like Mark Hix, a chef friend who writes for the *Independent*. He made me promise I wouldn't use it in one of my TV programmes when he took me there. However, Matthew Fort discovered it and wrote about it in his food column in the *Guardian*, so now I think my silence can be ended. We filmed there last autumn, mainly because of the long charcoal barbecue called a *mangal*, right at the front of the restaurant. Two muscular Turks sit behind it, chopping parsley, tomatoes and onions and feeding the grill with koftas moulded on to skewers, lamb kebabs, chops, whole quails, chicken wings, chillies and aubergines. The *mangal* gives off wreathes of smoke that are sucked greedily into a chimney above as you gaze through the window outside. It insists on you coming in and joining in the excitement.

turkish kofta kebabs with minted yogurt and kohlrabi and carrot salad

SERVES 4

900 g (2 lb) minced lamb
2 onions, finely grated
6 garlic cloves, crushed
2 teaspoons dried chilli flakes
1 small bunch of flat-leaf parsley, chopped
Oil for brushing
2 vine-ripened tomatoes, thinly sliced
Salt and freshly ground black pepper

FOR THE MINTED YOGURT:
200 g (7 oz) Greek natural yogurt
2 tablespoons chopped mint

FOR THE KOHLRABI AND CARROT SALAD:
2 large carrots, peeled and halved
2 kohlrabi, peeled
2 tablespoons sunflower oil
4 teaspoons cumin seeds
4 teaspoons lemon juice

1 If you are using a charcoal barbecue, light it 30–40 minutes before you want to start cooking. If using a gas barbecue, light it 10 minutes beforehand. If you are using a ridged cast-iron griddle, leave it to get hot over a high heat, then lower the heat slightly a few minutes before cooking. Cover 8 bamboo skewers with cold water and leave them to soak.

2 Put the minced lamb into a bowl with the onions, garlic, chilli flakes, parsley, 1 teaspoon of salt and some freshly ground black pepper. Mix together well with your hands until the mixture has bound together. Divide the mixture into 8 and then mould it into long sausage shapes around the drained bamboo skewers.

3 For the minted yogurt, mix the yogurt with the mint, ½ teaspoon of salt and some pepper and set aside.

4 For the salad, finely shred the carrots and kohlrabi, on a mandolin or on the coleslaw setting of your food processor so that you get nice long, thin, crunchy strips. Put them into a bowl with a large pinch of salt and mix together well. Heat the oil in a small pan, add the cumin seeds and, as soon as they start to sizzle, add them to the vegetables with the lemon juice and toss once more.

5 Brush the kofta generously with oil and lightly oil the bars of the barbecue or the griddle. Cook for 5 minutes, turning them now and them, until browned all over and cooked through.

6 Spread the minted yogurt over 1 large or 4 individual serving plates. Lay the kofta kebabs on top, garnish with the sliced tomatoes and serve with the kohlrabi and carrot salad.

It's very rare to find a vindaloo in the UK that tastes anything like the fragrant, slightly sharp curries of Goa. The word is actually spelt *vindalho* in Goa and refers to the main flavours of the original dish which were *vinho* (vinegar) and *alhos* (garlic), neither of which seem to appear very often, if at all, in the dish over here. Instead it's always just blindingly hot, flavoured with lots of raw-tasting curry powder. The Goan original calls for a large number of dried Kashmiri chillies, which are hot but not uncomfortably so. They are essential and give the dish a lovely deep red colour, making you think there's probably lots of tomato in it when in fact there's none in this recipe at all. However, do reduce the amount of fresh red chillies if you wish, to suit your taste, and even remove the seeds if you prefer.

pork vindaloo

SERVES 6

1 kg (2^{1}/$_{4}$ lb) boneless pork leg meat, cut
into 4 cm (1^{1}/$_{2}$ inch) pieces
200 ml (7 fl oz) red wine vinegar
100 g (4 oz) mild, dried red chillies, such
as Kashmiri, guajillo or New Mexico
1 heaped tablespoon cumin seeds
1 tablespoon cloves
10 cm (4 inch) piece of cinnamon stick,
broken in half
1 tablespoon black peppercorns
75 g (3 oz) medium-hot red Dutch
chillies, stalks removed and
roughly chopped
50 g (2 oz) garlic, peeled
2.5 cm (1 inch) piece of fresh ginger
A walnut-sized piece of tamarind pulp,
without the seeds
1 tablespoon light soft brown sugar
120 ml (4 fl oz) sunflower oil
2 onions, finely chopped
300 ml (10 fl oz) water
Salt
Steamed rice (see page 198) and pickles,
to serve

1 Put the diced pork into a bowl with half the vinegar and 1 teaspoon of salt. Mix together well and set aside for 20 minutes. Slit open the dried chillies and remove the stalks and seeds. Put the chillies into a bowl, cover with plenty of hot water and leave to soak for 20 minutes. Put the dried spices into a spice grinder and grind them to a fine powder.

2 Drain the pork, discarding the leftover vinegar, and dry well on kitchen paper. Drain the soaked chillies, put them into a liquidiser or food processor with the remaining vinegar and process to a smooth paste. Press through a sieve into a bowl to remove all the pieces of chilli skin and then return the paste to the cleaned food processor. Add the ground spices, fresh red chillies, garlic, ginger, tamarind and sugar and blend to a smooth paste.

3 Heat half the oil in a flameproof casserole or large saucepan. Fry the pork in batches until well browned on all sides. Transfer to a plate, add the rest of the oil to the pan with the onions and fry them for 20–30 minutes, until richly browned.

4 Add the vindaloo paste to the onions and fry for 5 minutes. Return the pork to the pan with the water and 1½ teaspoons of salt. Bring to the boil, then cover and simmer for 1–1½ hours, stirring now and then, until the pork is tender. Serve with some steamed basmati rice and pickles.

To write a recipe for something as everyday as roasting a joint of pork might seem the ultimate in teaching your grandmother to suck eggs but, while on the subject of eggs, I never thought it was arrogant of Delia Smith to go back over how to cook them properly. The fact is that most of us get the most straightforward of cooking operations wrong simply because we don't understand what's going on in the cooking process. That's why a book such as *On Food and Cooking* by Harold McGee (Prentice, Hall and IBD, 1997) was such a revelation. For the first time, somebody actually bothered to apply scientific principles to operations such as searing meat, and came up with the startling fact that searing does not seal.

So what are we looking for in a perfect joint of roast pork? The answer, of course, is crisp and aromatic crackling of a delicacy and crisp airiness that words cannot describe. The enemy of crackling is moisture and this comes from two sources: first, from damp skin and second, from the meat juices themselves. As a butcher friend of mine observed, plastic is the enemy of pork. If your joint of pork comes recently shrink-wrapped it will never produce crackling. Pork needs to be hung for a couple of days in a well-aerated fridge so that the skin has time to dry out, and this is precisely why the Chinese hang up their ducks for a good crisp skin. The other source of moisture during the roasting process is the meat itself, and in order to get good crackling you need a thick layer of fat under the skin to separate the flesh from it. Sadly most lean-bred supermarket pork will never give you good crackling because it just doesn't have enough fat. The best joints of pork for crackling are spare rib and loin. You will never get crackling from roasting a leg because there is too much lean and not enough fat.

The process of scoring pork also helps to improve the quality of the crackling, allowing the fat to bubble up through the cuts to make the skin crisp, as well as making it easier to break up after cooking. But if you score too deeply through the skin and fat into the flesh, you will encourage the moisture in the meat to soften the crackling.

I always prefer to roast any meat on the bone and it is particularly easy with pork – just get your butcher to chine the joint, i. e. cut the backbone from the ribs but leave both in place. It is a simple matter prior to carving to run your knife down the ribs and over the spine to remove the cushion of meat.

roast pork

SERVES 6

1.75 kg (4 lb) boned and rolled spare rib
of pork (the shoulder joint,
not the belly)
Sunflower oil
The bones from the joint (optional)
1 teaspoon plain flour
Salt and freshly ground black pepper
Roast potatoes (see page 194), *Sautéed
red cabbage with pears* (see page
196) or *Steamed greens* (see
page 196), to serve

1 Put your joint of pork on a rack set over a dish or small roasting tin and leave it somewhere cool and airy for 24 hours, so the skin can dry off.

2 The next day, preheat your oven to the highest possible setting. Season the cut faces of the pork with salt and pepper but leave the skin untouched. Take a large roasting tin, big enough to hold the joint and a generous serving of potatoes, and coat the base with a thin film of oil. Put the bones, if you have them, into the centre of the tin to act as a trivet and put the joint on top, skin-side up. Put in the oven and roast for 20 minutes, then lower the oven temperature to 180°C/350°F/Gas Mark 4 and continue to roast for 30 minutes per 450 g (1 lb) – so a 1.75 kg (4 lb) joint will take a further 2 hours.

3 Refer to the recipe on page 194 for the roast potatoes. Boil them as soon as you lower the oven temperature for the pork, then drain,

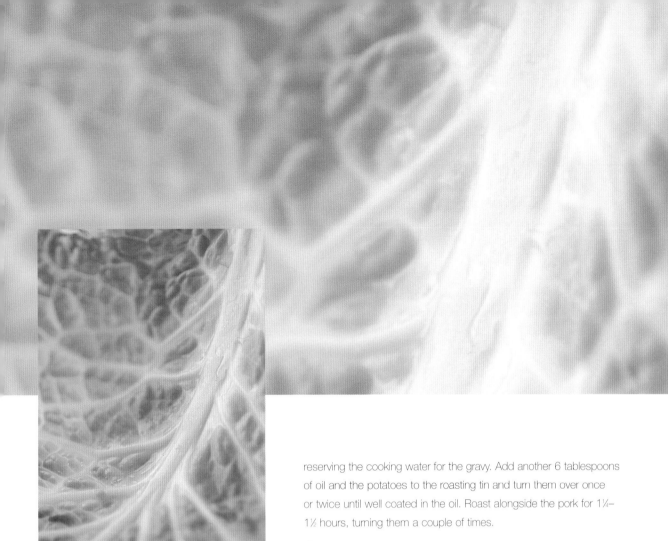

reserving the cooking water for the gravy. Add another 6 tablespoons of oil and the potatoes to the roasting tin and turn them over once or twice until well coated in the oil. Roast alongside the pork for 1¼– 1½ hours, turning them a couple of times.

4 Remove the pork from the oven – a meat thermometer pushed into the centre of the joint should register 75°C/170°F. Transfer it to a board and leave to rest somewhere warm for 10 minutes, during which time the internal temperature should rise to 80°C/180°F. If the potatoes are not quite brown enough, transfer them to a small roasting tin and return them to the oven whilst the pork is resting and you make the gravy.

5 For the gravy, pour off the excess fat from the tin and put the tin over a medium heat. Add the flour and stir it around in the residue, allowing it to brown a little. Add 600 ml (1 pint) of the reserved potato cooking water and scrape the base of the tin with a wooden spoon to loosen all the caramelised juices. Bring to the boil and boil for a few minutes, until you have a good gravy-like consistency. Strain into a warmed sauceboat and adjust the seasoning if necessary.

6 To carve, cut and remove the string, slide a knife under the crackling, lift it off and break it into pieces. Carve the pork across into thin slices and arrange them on a warmed serving plate with the crackling and roast potatoes. Serve with the gravy and red cabbage or steamed greens.

Do you ever crave for those incredibly simple terrines that you can buy in charcuteries all over France, which taste of just pork, herbs and spices? They often come in big rectangular dishes, from which they are sliced and wrapped in waxed paper. Somehow, the recipes for terrines that I find in books over here never seem to produce a flavour that is straightforward and fresh. Maybe it's all that marinating in wine and liqueurs, and careful layering of different textures. This recipe, which Debbie made for our working lunches whilst we were writing the book, seems to capture exactly what I'm looking for. It's just pork belly, a little liver, bacon and plenty of herbs with some garlic, onion and seasoning, and you can knock it up in 20 minutes. Do, however, try to get hold of a nice, wide terrine dish in which to cook it because it will look so much better when you come to serve it.

coarse pork-and-herb terrine

SERVES 10

2 tablespoons olive oil
175 g (6 oz) onions, finely chopped
1 kg (2¼ lb) rindless boned pork belly, cut into small pieces
175 g (6 oz) rindless back bacon, cut into small pieces
175 g (6 oz) lamb's or pig's liver, cut into small pieces
2 small garlic cloves, finely chopped
A large handful of parsley leaves, finely chopped
1½ tablespoons chopped rosemary
1½ tablespoons chopped thyme
1½ teaspoons salt and 1½ teaspoons freshly ground black pepper
Pickled blueberries (see page 198), Beetroot chutney (see page 198), cornichons and crusty bread, to serve

1 Heat the oil in a frying pan, add the onions and fry gently until soft but not browned. Transfer to a large mixing bowl and leave to cool.

2 Put the pork belly into a food processor and chop, using the pulse button, into a coarse but not too coarse mixture. Add to the onions in the bowl. Put the bacon and liver in the food processor and again, coarsely chop, then transfer to the bowl.

3 Add the garlic, chopped herbs, salt and pepper and mix everything together really well – the best way of distributing the ingredients evenly is with your hands.

4 Preheat the oven to 180°C/350°F/Gas Mark 4. Put the mixture into a lightly oiled 1.5 litre (2½ pint) terrine dish or loaf tin and slightly round off the top. Cover with a lid or some foil, put into a small roasting tin and pour enough hot water into the tin to come half way up the sides of the dish. Bake for 1½ hours.

5 Uncover the terrine and cook for a further 15 minutes, until it is lightly coloured on top. Remove the dish from the roasting tin and leave to cool, then weight down the terrine overnight in the fridge. The easiest way to do this is to cut out a piece of cardboard that will fit inside the rim of the dish, cover it with foil, then place it on top of the terrine and place a few weights or unopened cans on top.

6 To serve, remove the terrine from the dish in slices. Accompany with lots of crusty bread, the pickled blueberries, beetroot chutney and some cornichons.

We have all now changed our eating habits. Our tolerance of butter and cream is much reduced and I don't know anybody who drinks full cream milk any more. A dish like this, which would have been perfection in the seventies, would now taste rich and overpowering after one or two mouthfuls. But the combination of a lean meat such as pork and the emollience of cream with the sweetness of prunes is a good one. So I've merely re-written the recipe with less fat and I think you'll find it is all the better for it. Even so, I would not suggest you eat this except at lunchtime after some prolonged exercise or a walk on Bodmin Moor on a cold winter's day, encompassing Rough Tor and Brown Willy, after which no dish would seem more appropriate. Serve with some small pasta shapes, moistened with a little butter, and a simple green salad.

pork with cream and prunes

SERVES 4

12 no-need-to-soak prunes,
such as Agen
300 ml (10 fl oz) *Chicken stock*
(see page 200)
150 ml (5 fl oz) dry white wine
4 x 175 g (6 oz) thick pork loin steaks
25 g (1 oz) plain flour
1 tablespoon sunflower oil
4 tablespoons crème fraîche
25 g (1 oz) unsalted butter, cut
into small pieces
A small handful of parsley,
finely chopped
Salt and freshly ground black pepper
Cooked small pasta shapes and *Light green salad* (page 197), to serve

1 Put the prunes into a small pan with the chicken stock and wine. Bring to the boil and simmer for 5 minutes or until tender. Lift them out on to a plate, cover and set aside. Reserve the cooking liquor.

2 Trim any rind and the excess fat from each pork steak. Season on both sides with salt and pepper and then lightly coat with the flour, patting off the excess.

3 Heat the oil in a large frying pan, add the steaks and fry gently for 5 minutes on each side, until lightly golden and cooked through. Transfer to a warm serving dish, scatter the cooked prunes around, cover with foil and keep warm in a low oven.

4 Pour away any excess oil from the frying pan, add the prune cooking liquor and boil rapidly until reduced by three-quarters and well concentrated in flavour. Lower the heat and whisk in the crème fraîche and butter; the sauce should be thick enough to coat the back of a wooden spoon lightly.

5 Remove the pork from the oven and pour the sauce over it. Scatter with the chopped parsley and serve with some cooked pasta and the green salad.

My enthusiasm for toad-in-the-hole began in the early days of the Seafood Restaurant, when one of our chefs, Dave Miney, a really good cook and now head chef at the Oxo Tower on London's South Bank, would make the most superb Derbyshire toad-in-the-hole on a Saturday night after service. It was to go with the large number of beers we would be knocking back because we knew we had got the Sunday off. I've thrown a handful of dried porcini mushrooms into the gravy to increase the beefy flavour.

toad-in-the-hole with porcini mushroom and onion gravy

SERVES 4

175 g (6 oz) plain flour
1/4 teaspoon salt
2 medium eggs
175 ml (6 fl oz) full-cream milk
120 ml (4 fl oz) cold water
450 g (1 lb) good-quality pork sausages
5 tablespoons sunflower oil

FOR THE PORCINI MUSHROOM AND
ONION GRAVY:
25 g (1 oz) unsalted butter
450 g (1 lb) onions, thinly sliced
1/2 teaspoon sugar
1 tablespoon plain flour
600 ml (1 pint) *Beef broth* (see page 200)
15 g (1/2 oz) dried porcini mushrooms
1 tablespoon Worcestershire sauce
1/2 teaspoon English mustard
1 teaspoon thyme leaves
Salt and freshly ground black pepper

1 For the gravy, heat the butter in a large frying pan, add the onions and sugar and cook over a medium heat for 20–30 minutes, until soft and richly caramelised. Stir in the flour, cook for a few seconds, then add the beef stock, porcini mushrooms, Worcestershire sauce, mustard, thyme leaves, salt and pepper. Simmer for 20 minutes.

2 For the batter, sift the flour and salt into a bowl, make a well in the centre and break in the eggs. Gradually add the milk and water, whisking everything together into a smooth batter. Set aside for 15 minutes.

3 Preheat the oven to 220°C/425°F/Gas Mark 7. Fry the sausages in 1 tablespoon of the oil until nicely browned all over.

4 Put the remaining oil into a cast-iron dish or reliably non-stick roasting tin measuring about 28 x 20 cm (11 x 8 inches) and heat it in the oven for 5 minutes. Remove the hot tin from the oven, tilt it to coat the base and sides with the oil, then add the sausages. Briefly re-whisk the batter and pour it over the sausages. Return the tin to the top shelf of the oven as quickly as you can and cook for 30–35 minutes, until the batter is puffed up and golden. Remove the toad in the hole from the oven, cut into portions and serve with the gravy.

I didn't exactly make this dish up. Not so long ago I was in a restaurant in Norcia in Umbria – a town famed for its pork butchers – and ordered a plate of sausage and lentils. The sausage came coiled like a Cumberland sausage, only smaller, and the lentils, which I discovered grew on a plain just above Norcia, were tiny like Puy lentils, with a delightful earthy, nutty flavour. As far as I could make out, the lentils had lots of chilli and rosemary and red wine with them – probably the same wine as I drank with the dish. This recipe is pretty close to what I ate and makes great use of Austin Davis's brilliant, meaty sausages (available by mail order from Border County Foods, tel: 01228 573500).

cumberland sausage with red wine, rosemary and lentils

SERVES 4

225 g (8 oz) Umbrian lentils or
Puy lentils
1 x 675 g (1¹/₂ lb) Cumberland sausage
3 tablespoons olive oil
300 ml (10 fl oz) red wine
2 garlic cloves, finely chopped
2 shallots, finely chopped
Leaves from 2 sprigs of rosemary
A small handful of small sage leaves
1 red chilli, seeded and chopped
6 sun-dried tomatoes in oil, drained and
cut across into thin strips
300 ml (10 fl oz) *Beef broth* (see
page 200)
2 tablespoons chopped flat-leaf parsley
Salt and freshly ground black pepper

1 Add the lentils to a pan of boiling salted water and cook for about 15 minutes, until they are tender but still have a little bite left in them. They will be cooked a little more later on. Drain and set aside.

2 Pass 2 large metal skewers diagonally through the sausage to help it keep its shape during cooking. Brush the base of a large, deep frying pan with 1 tablespoon of the oil and place it over a medium heat. When hot, add the sausage and fry it for 8–10 minutes, turning it over halfway through, until nicely browned on both sides and cooked through. Transfer to a baking tray, cover loosely with foil and keep hot in a low oven.

3 Pour the excess oil out of the pan, return the pan to the heat and add the red wine. Increase the heat and allow the wine to boil vigorously until reduced to about 3 tablespoons. Pour this reduction into a bowl and set aside.

4 Heat the remaining oil in the pan, add the garlic, shallots, rosemary, sage and chilli and fry over a medium-high heat until the shallots are soft and lightly browned. Add the sun-dried tomatoes, lentils, red wine reduction, beef broth and some salt and pepper and simmer gently until the liquid has reduced slightly and the lentils are tender.

5 Stir the chopped parsley into the lentils and spoon them into a warmed shallow serving dish. Put the Cumberland sausage on top and remove the skewers to serve.

6 furred and

ONE OF THE EXPERIENCES I ENJOYED MOST DURING THE FILMING OF *FOOD HEROES* WAS JOINING A COUPLE OF GAME SHOOTS. THE KNOWLEDGE OF LOCAL WILDLIFE AND THE SENSITIVITY TO THE BALANCE OF NATURE IN THE COUNTRYSIDE SHOWN BY THOSE I MET WAS WONDERFUL. THIS WAS THE CASE BOTH WITH A GROUP OF LOCAL FARMERS I MET OUTSIDE WADEBRIDGE IN CORNWALL, AND THE PEOPLE I MET ON ONE OF THE MOST FAMOUS ESTATES IN THE COUNTRY, HOLKHAM IN NORFOLK. THE HEAD GAMEKEEPER THERE, SIMON MINCHIN, UNDERSTOOD THE DIFFICULTY PEOPLE HAD IN MARRYING SHOOTING WITH CONSERVATION BUT, AS HE POINTED OUT, 'SHOOTING IS THE HARVESTING OF OUR CROP.' THOSE WILD, GREY-LEGGED PARTRIDGES THAT FORAGED FOR FOOD FROM SET-ASIDE LAND, TASTED SUBLIME.

feathered game

A partridge and
pheasant shoot near
Louth, Lincolnshire.

The beetroot recipe for this dish comes from one of my food heroes, Edouard de Pomiane, a gourmet of the early twentieth century who wrote cookery books renowned for their humorous style and approachable recipes. Even today it is rare to find a cookery writer with so much common sense, who was also so dedicated to explaining to his readers why and how things happened in cooking.

venison steaks au poivre with hot beetroot and horseradish

SERVES 4

1¹/₂ tablespoons black peppercorns
4 x 175–200 g (6–7 oz) topside leg steaks of venison, cut 4 cm (1¹/₂ inches) thick
3 tablespoons olive oil
25 g (1 oz) unsalted butter
1 tablespoon Cognac
120 ml (4 fl oz) *Beef broth* (see page 200) or *Chicken stock* (see page 200)
Plain boiled new potatoes (see page 194), to serve

FOR THE HOT BEETROOT AND HORSERADISH:
675 g (1¹/₂ lb) raw beetroot
2 tablespoons sunflower oil
25 g (1 oz) butter
2 tablespoons red wine vinegar
1 teaspoon caster sugar
2 teaspoons finely grated horseradish (from a jar or fresh)
50 ml (2 fl oz) double cream
Salt and freshly ground black pepper

1 Preheat the oven to 200°C/400°F/Gas Mark 6. Trim the beetroot of their leaves and roots and put them into a small roasting tin with the oil. Roast for 40 minutes or until tender when pierced with the tip of a small knife. Leave until cool enough to handle, then peel and cut into 1 cm (½ inch) dice. This can be done some time beforehand, if you wish.

2 For the venison, coarsely crush the peppercorns in a pestle and mortar and then tip them into a small sieve and shake well to remove all the very fine pepper powder. Transfer what's left in the sieve to a small baking tray and push both sides of each steak briefly into it so that they become evenly coated. Season on both sides with a little salt.

3 To finish the beetroot, melt the butter in a pan, add the beetroot, vinegar, sugar, horseradish, cream and some seasoning and heat through gently for 2–3 minutes. Cover and keep warm.

4 Heat the olive oil in a large frying pan, add the venison steaks and fry for 3 minutes, until well coloured. Turn over and add 15 g (½ oz) of the butter and the Cognac to the pan. Cook for a further 3 minutes, then transfer to a warmed serving plate, cover and keep warm in a low oven.

5 Add the stock to the frying pan and scrape the base with a wooden spoon to loosen all the caramelised juices. Simmer for 3–4 minutes, until reduced and well flavoured, then whisk in the remaining butter.

6 Place the steaks on 4 warmed plates and spoon some of the beetroot alongside. Pour the sauce over and serve with the new potatoes.

The ability to choose between a tender and succulent wild rabbit and a tough, sinewy old one is unfortunately an almost impossible task unless you are lucky enough to know a reliable butcher or game dealer who knows his stuff. Otherwise you'd be much better off buying humanely farmed domestic rabbit. This cacciatora is so well known that it is almost impossible to pin down a definitive recipe. I like unpeeled cloves of garlic and lots of sage, rosemary and oregano fried in the olive oil before adding the rabbit and a small quantity of a very concentrated, intensely flavoured tomato sauce with black olives and a little chilli. It is equally good made with chicken.

rabbit cacciatora with grilled parmesan polenta

SERVES 4

3 tablespoons olive oil
1 head of garlic, separated into cloves
10 sage leaves
The leaves from 1 sprig of rosemary
2 sprigs of oregano or thyme
1 rabbit, jointed into 8
120 ml (4 fl oz) dry white wine
400 g (14 oz) can of chopped tomatoes
12 small black olives
A pinch of dried chilli flakes
Salt and freshly ground black pepper
A small handful of coarsely chopped
parsley, to garnish

FOR THE GRILLED PARMESAN POLENTA:
900 ml (1¹/₂ pints) water
150 g (5 oz) polenta
25 g (1 oz) Parmesan cheese,
freshly grated

1 For the polenta, bring the water to the boil in a medium-sized pan and then add the polenta in a slow, steady stream, stirring all the time. Lower the heat and simmer gently for 20 minutes, stirring frequently. Stir in the Parmesan cheese and ¾ teaspoon of salt and pour the mixture into a lightly oiled 25 x 18 cm (10 x 7 inch) shallow rectangular tin. Leave for 3–4 hours, until completely cold and set.

2 For the cacciatora, heat the olive oil and unpeeled garlic cloves in a large, shallow pan and fry for 3–4 minutes, until the garlic is lightly browned. Add the sage, rosemary and oregano or thyme and fry for another minute. Lower the heat slightly, add the rabbit pieces and fry until lightly browned all over.

3 Add the white wine to the pan and cook until reduced to a couple of tablespoons. Stir in the tomatoes, black olives, chilli flakes, 1 teaspoon of salt and 20 turns of the black peppermill. Cover and simmer for 30 minutes or until the rabbit is tender, then uncover the pan, increase the heat slightly and cook until the sauce has reduced, thickened and become concentrated in flavour.

4 Shortly before the rabbit is cooked, turn the polenta out on to a board and cut it into 8 pieces. Heat a large, dry, non-stick frying pan over a high heat, add the pieces of polenta and fry for 2–3 minutes on each side, until lightly golden. Overlap 2 pieces of polenta on each of 4 warmed plates, spoon the rabbit alongside and serve.

Matthew Fort is a serious food writer and great friend. He found this dish in Piedmont while on a reflective tour from the tip of Southern Italy to Turin in the north – on a Vespa, would you believe? It's exactly the kind of food I love and so does he: rabbit, which is poor man's food, cooked somewhere in the middle of the country to taste like the best tuna. It expresses the ingenuity of agricultural communities living far from the sea. Fresh sea fish would have been unobtainable, tinned tuna expensive. Rabbit, on the other hand, was relatively cheap and readily available. It is poached until tender, taken off the bone and then marinated in olive oil, with garlic and herbs for a few days. By then the meat will have taken on that particular firm, flaky texture of tuna and absorbed the flavour of the garlic and herbs. Matthew serves it on garlic bruschetta with some rocket leaves and a few drops of saba or balsamic vinegar. Saba is a concentrated grape juice and is available from good Italian delicatessens.

matthew fort's tonno di coniglio (rabbit cooked like tuna)

SERVES 6 OR MORE

1 rabbit, jointed into 6 pieces
A small bunch each of thyme, sage and
bay leaves
5 garlic cloves, sliced
About 1 litre (1¾ pints) inexpensive
olive oil
Salt and freshly ground black pepper

FOR THE BRUSCHETTA:
About 12 slices of ciabatta or French
stick, cut 1 cm (½ inch) thick
2 garlic cloves, peeled
50 g (2 oz) rocket
A little good-quality saba or
balsamic vinegar
A little freshly squeezed lemon juice
Maldon sea salt flakes and freshly
ground black pepper

1 Put the rabbit into a large pan and cover it with well-salted water (i.e. 1 teaspoon salt per 600 ml/1 pint of water). Bring to a simmer and leave to cook gently for 1½ –2 hours until the meat is ready to fall off the bone. Lift the pieces of rabbit out of the liquid and, when they are cool enough to handle, pull the flesh off the bones.

2 In a large, deep container, such as a glass bowl or an earthenware pot, layer the rabbit with the herbs and garlic, seasoning the layers with salt and pepper. You should have at least 3 layers of rabbit. Pour over the olive oil so that the rabbit is completely submerged. Cover and place in the fridge for at least 5 days, but you can keep it for up to 2 weeks.

3 To serve, you can do one of two things. For larger numbers, remove the bowl from the fridge and leave it to come back to room temperature so that the olive oil becomes liquid again. Alternatively, if you don't want to use it all at once, lift some of the rabbit out of the oil and cover the remainder once again with the chilled olive oil to make good the seal.

4 Toast the slices of bread until lightly golden on both sides. Rub one side of each piece with the peeled garlic cloves and then top each one with some rocket leaves. Top the leaves with some of the rabbit, sprinkle with a few drops of saba or balsamic vinegar, a little lemon, a few sea salt flakes and some black pepper and serve straight away.

I'm often rather depressed in restaurants to be served squab. It normally comes pan-fried and pink, with the inevitable heavily reduced veal jus, giving you that tacky taste of boiled hooves. Whenever I see the word 'jus' on a menu, my heart sinks. It's almost as if pigeon breasts have been reduced to the role of more red meat to accompany the chefs' over-skilful sauces. I'm not always averse to cooking the breasts of poultry and game birds on their own but the flavour is so much better when they are roasted on the bone. In this recipe you can either remove the breasts after roasting, as I have done, or serve the whole bird. I've accompanied the squabs (which are tender young pigeons) with rather a nice potato tart – which is a little bit 'cheffy', I do concede, but well worth the effort. You can make the tarts up some time beforehand and keep them chilled in the fridge until you are ready to cook them.

roasted squab with potato, bacon and truffle oil pithiviers

SERVES 4

4 fresh bay leaves
4 sprigs of thyme
4 squabs (young pigeon)
8 rashers of rindless streaky bacon
Salt and freshly ground black pepper
Steamed greens (see page 196), to serve

FOR THE POTATO, BACON AND TRUFFLE OIL PITHIVIERS:
600 ml (1 pint) *Chicken stock* (see page 200)
4 x 75 g (3 oz) floury potatoes, such as Maris Piper, peeled and cut into slices 5 mm (¼ inch) thick
50 g (2 oz) onion, thinly sliced
1 garlic clove, finely chopped
The leaves from 1 sprig of thyme
25 g (1 oz) bacon lardons (short, fat strips)
500 g (1 lb 2 oz) chilled puff pastry
2 teaspoons truffle oil
1 egg, beaten

1 For the pithiviers, put the chicken stock into a saucepan, bring to the boil and boil rapidly until reduced by half. Add the potato slices with the onion, garlic, thyme leaves, bacon, ½ teaspoon of salt and some black pepper and simmer for 5 minutes, until the potatoes are just tender. Tip into a sieve set over a bowl to collect the remaining stock and leave to cool. Reserve the stock.

2 Roll out the pastry on a lightly floured surface and cut out four 10 cm (4 inch) discs and four 12.5 cm (5 inch) discs. Put the smaller discs of pastry on to a greased baking sheet and layer the potatoes, onion, bacon and a little seasoning on top of each one, leaving a 1 cm (½ inch) border free around the edge. Drizzle over the truffle oil. Brush the edges of the pastry with beaten egg and cover with the larger discs of pastry, pressing the edges together well to seal. Chill for at least 20 minutes.

3 Preheat the oven to 200°C/400°F/Gas Mark 6. Brush the top of the pithiviers with beaten egg and then, with the tip of a small, sharp knife, score radiating arcs from the centre out towards the edge, just into the surface of the pastry – be careful not to cut right through. Make a small hole in the centre of each pie to allow the steam to escape.

4 Put a bay leaf and sprig of thyme inside each squab, wrap each bird in 2 rashers of bacon so that the breast is protected and put them into a small roasting tin. Put the pithiviers and squab into the oven and cook for 25 minutes. Remove both from the oven, take the bacon off the squab and return the birds to the oven for 5 minutes to brown the skin lightly.

5 Remove the squab from the oven, place them on a board, cover tightly with foil and leave to rest. Turn off the oven and put the pithiviers back in to keep warm. Pour away any excess fat from the roasting tin and strain in the reserved stock from the pithiviers. Bring to the boil, scraping the base of the tin with a wooden spoon to release all the caramelised juices. Simmer for 2–3 minutes, season to taste and strain into a small pan and leave over a low heat.

6 Uncover the squab and carve the breast meat away from each bird if you wish. Put the squab and bacon on to 4 warmed plates with a pithivier alongside. Pour over the gravy and serve with some steamed greens.

This is my imaginative idea of Spanish food: clean, but excitingly spicy. And nothing epitomises my romantic thoughts of fiery Spanish cooking more than chorizo, the hot-smoked paprika, chilli and garlic sausage that appears in dishes such as lima beans, snails, hake *cazuelas* and paella. The quails are spatchcocked and held open with skewers, then cooked on a char-grill with some chunky potato wedges brushed with olive oil. And served with a vibrant salad of tomatoes, roasted red peppers and green chillies, preferably arranged on a Spaghetti-Western-style platter.

grilled spiced quail with olive oil potatoes and tomato and hot red pepper salad

SERVES 4

8 x 100–150 g (4–5 oz) prepared quail
25 g (1 oz) chorizo, skinned and
roughly chopped
2 garlic cloves, roughly chopped
$^1/_2$ teaspoon dried chilli flakes
$^1/_2$ teaspoon sweet paprika
1–2 tablespoons olive oil
Salt and freshly ground black pepper

FOR THE OLIVE OIL POTATOES:
550 g (1$^1/_4$ lb) large, floury potatoes,
such as Maris Piper
1 tablespoon olive oil
1 large garlic clove, crushed

FOR THE TOMATO AND HOT RED
PEPPER SALAD:
1 *Roasted red pepper* (see page 201)
2 large beef tomatoes, thinly sliced
1 medium-hot green Dutch chilli,
seeded and chopped
1 garlic clove, finely chopped
A large handful of flat-leaf parsley
leaves, chopped
2 teaspoons lemon juice
3 tablespoons extra virgin olive oil

1 To spatchcock the quail, turn each one breast-side down and cut along either side of the backbone with scissors. Discard the backbone, open the bird out, turn it over and press down firmly on the breastbone to flatten it. Rinse the birds under cold running water to clean the cavities and remove any remaining feathers. Pat dry with kitchen paper.

2 Put the chorizo into a food processor and process briefly, using the pulse button, until finely chopped. Add the garlic, dried chilli flakes, paprika, ½ teaspoon of salt and enough olive oil to be able to blend everything together into a smooth paste.

3 Carefully ease your fingers under the skin of each bird to loosen it, taking care not to tear it, and spread some of the chorizo–chilli paste under the skin. Push the skin back into place and then pass 2 fine metal skewers diagonally through each bird to keep it flat.

4 For the olive oil potatoes, cut each unpeeled potato lengthways into 8 wedges. Put them into a bowl with the oil, garlic and some seasoning and toss together until evenly coated.

5 If you are using a charcoal barbecue, light it 30–40 minutes before you want to cook on it. If you are using a gas barbecue, light it 10 minutes beforehand. If you are using a ridged cast-iron griddle, leave it to get hot over a high heat 2–3 minutes before you are ready to cook, then reduce the heat to medium.

6 Meanwhile, put together the salad. Remove the stalk, skin and seeds from the roasted pepper and cut it into long, thin strips. Arrange the sliced tomatoes on a serving plate and sprinkle with some salt and pepper. Scatter over the red pepper strips, green chilli, garlic, parsley, lemon juice and olive oil.

7 Brush the outside of the quail with oil, season with some salt and pepper and put skin-side down on the barbecue or griddle. Cook over a medium heat for 5 minutes, until they have taken on a good colour, then turn them over. Add the potato wedges cut-face down and cook for 5–6 minutes. Turn the potatoes and the quails once more and cook for a further 5–6 minutes, until the potatoes are golden brown on both sides and the quail are cooked through.

8 Place the quail on a warmed serving platter. Put the olive oil potatoes in a warmed serving dish, sprinkle with some sea salt flakes and take both to the table with the salad.

As I've said before, what can you do with the ubiquitous pheasant? They are now so common, and frankly can be disappointing unless you get a wild bird that has been properly handled. Nevertheless, the flavour of any pheasant is good if sympathetically handled, and I think an oriental treatment works extremely well. In this recipe the birds are poached in a good chicken stock flavoured with star anise and chilli, then served in a deep bowl with some bok choi, coriander and finely shredded spring onions.

poached pheasant in a star anise and chilli broth with bok choi and udon noodles

SERVES 4

1.75 litres (3 pints) *Chicken stock*
(see page 200)
1/2 teaspoon Sichuan peppercorns
1/2 teaspoon dried chilli flakes
1/2 teaspoon black peppercorns
1/2 teaspoon fennel seeds
1/2 teaspoon cloves
2 star anise
2.5 cm (1 inch) piece of cinnamon stick
5 garlic cloves, sliced
1 brace of prepared pheasant
1 teaspoon salt

TO FINISH THE BROTH:
200 g (7 oz) fresh udon noodles
4 heads of bok choi, cut in half
lengthways through the stalk
2.5 cm (1 inch) piece of fresh ginger,
peeled and cut into fine julienne
1 medium-hot green Dutch chilli, halved,
seeded and cut into long, thin strips
4 spring onions, halved and
finely shredded
A handful of coriander leaves

1 Put the chicken stock and all the aromatic flavourings into a large pan in which the brace of pheasant will fit snugly. Bring to the boil, lower in the pheasant and add a little more water, if necessary, so that they are barely covered. Add the salt, bring back to the boil and simmer gently for 15–20 minutes or until the juices run clear when a thigh is pierced with a skewer.

2 Place the pheasants on a board. Strain the broth to remove the flavourings, return it to the pan and bring back to a simmer. Add the udon noodles, bok choi, ginger and chilli and simmer for 4 minutes.

3 Meanwhile, cut the legs off the pheasants and cut them in half at the joint. Cut the breast meat away from the birds in whole pieces.

4 To serve, divide the noodles and bok choi between 4 warmed, deep, bistro-style plates and place a piece of breast and leg meat on top of each. Ladle over the hot broth and sprinkle with the spring onions and coriander leaves.

There's not much I like doing with small, exquisite game birds such as partridge, woodcock, snipe or wild duck other than either roasting them and serving them up traditionally with bread sauce, redcurrant jelly and game chips, or pot-roasting them. The latter has the advantage of keeping what are essentially lean pieces of protein moist. The success of this dish lies in the flavourings of smoked bacon, cabbage and chestnuts. You can now buy really good vacuum-packed ready-peeled chestnuts, which have a very attractive flavour.

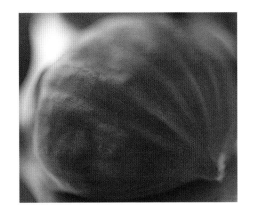

pot-roast partridge with cabbage and chestnuts

SERVES 4

1 tablespoon olive oil

4 small or 2 large prepared partridges

150 g (5 oz) smoked streaky bacon lardons (short, fat strips)

25 g (1 oz) butter

16 small shallots, peeled but left whole

8 small garlic cloves, peeled but left whole

2 carrots, cut into batons

2 bay leaves

150 ml (5 fl oz) *Chicken stock* (see page 200)

1 Savoy cabbage, outer leaves removed, then cut into 8 wedges through the core

200 g (7 oz) cooked peeled chestnuts

Salt and freshly ground black pepper

Plain boiled potatoes (see page 194) or *Mashed potatoes* (see page 194), to serve

1 Preheat the oven to 160°C/325°F/Gas Mark 3. Heat the oil in a flameproof casserole, add the partridges and brown them lightly all over. Lift the partridges on to a plate, add the bacon lardons to the pan and cook until lightly golden. Add the butter, shallots, garlic, carrots and bay leaves and cook over a medium heat until lightly coloured.

2 Return the partridges to the casserole with the stock, 1 teaspoon of salt and plenty of black pepper. Cover with a well-fitting lid, transfer to the oven and cook for 20–30 minutes, depending on the size of the birds.

3 Meanwhile, drop the wedges of cabbage into a pan of boiling salted water and blanch for 2–3 minutes. Drain, refresh under cold running water and drain once more. Set to one side.

4 Remove the casserole from the oven, take out the partridges, cover and leave to rest in a warm place. Add the cabbage and chestnuts to the casserole and turn them over once or twice in the cooking juices. Simmer on top of the stove for 5 minutes until the cabbage is cooked.

5 Divide the cabbage, chestnuts and braised vegetables between 4 warmed plates and place the birds on top. Serve with the potatoes.

7 desserts, cakes

DURING THE APPLE HARVEST IN THIS, THE WARMEST SUMMER FOR NEARLY 30 YEARS, TWO OF THE LARGEST SUPERMARKETS WERE SELLING TWO IMPORTED APPLES FOR EVERY BRITISH ONE. IN A COUNTRY THAT PROBABLY GROWS THE BEST-FLAVOURED APPLES IN THE WORLD, THIS IS CURIOUS. I RECALL, THIS SAME SEASON, EATING A WARWICKSHIRE DROOPER: A SWEET YELLOW PLUM WITH A FRAGRANCE REMINISCENT OF ITALIAN WHITE PEACHES, WHICH HARDLY EXISTS ANYMORE BECAUSE OF ITS UNSUITABILITY FOR RETAIL SALE. VARIETIES OF HOME-GROWN FRUIT SEEM EVER HARDER TO GET. THIS CHAPTER IS FULL OF RECIPES FOR FRUIT THAT SHOULD BE MORE POPULAR – GREENGAGES, DAMSONS, QUINCES, GOOSEBERRIES – AND LOTS MORE RECIPES FOR RATHER IRRESISTIBLE BRITISH AND IRISH PUDDINGS, CAKES AND BREADS, TOO.

and bread

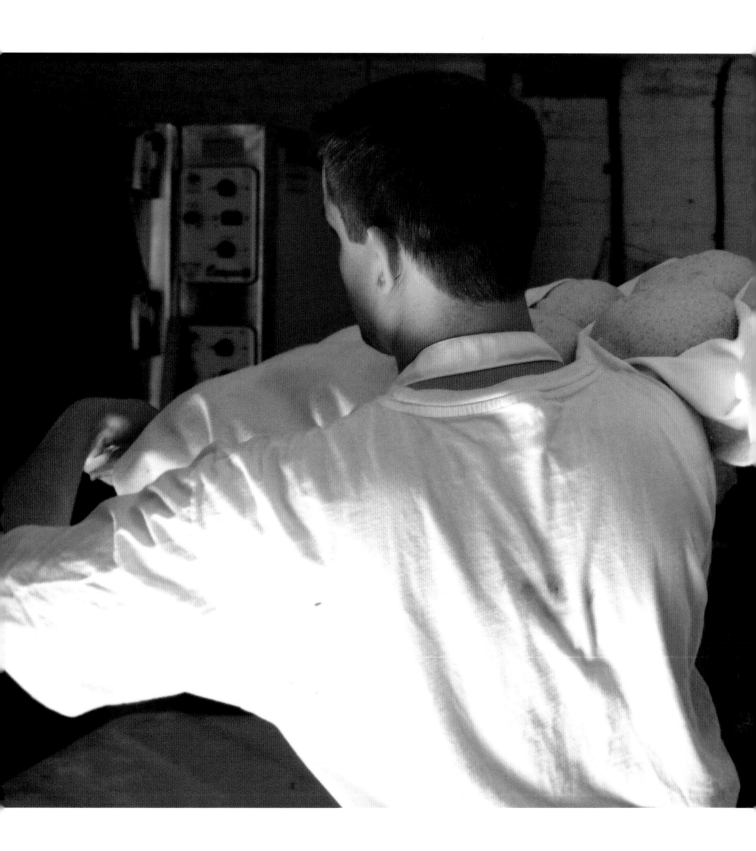

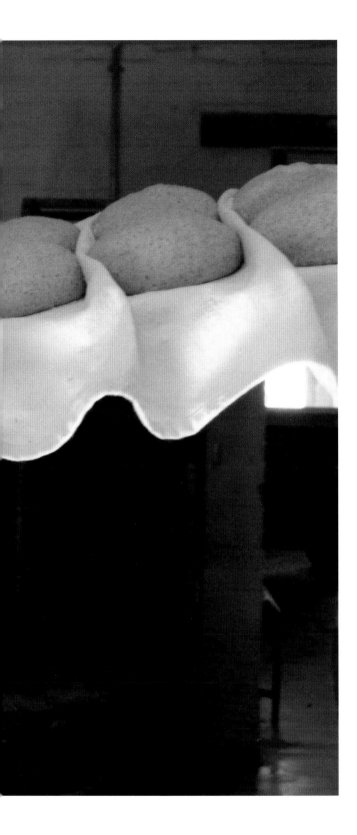

Bread making at Long Crichel bakery, Wimborne, Dorset. Here traditional techniques are used in the bread-making process, including baking the loaves in a wood-fired oven.

A small slice of Bakewell tart with a slippery, thick Italian coffee in some smart, relaxed café whilst reading the morning papers is pretty civilised, but as a pudding it doesn't quite work for me because it's just too rich. So I've layered the tart with some lightly poached raspberries and omitted the usual sugary-sweet glacé icing topping.

bakewell tart with fresh raspberries

SERVES 10–12

1 quantity of *Rich shortcrust pastry*
(see page 201)
350 g (12 oz) fresh raspberries
225 g (8 oz) caster sugar, plus extra
to decorate
3 medium eggs, beaten
100 g (4 oz) softened butter
75 g (3 oz) ground almonds
40 g (1$^{1}/_{2}$ oz) plain flour
2–3 drops of almond extract
Double cream, to serve

1 Roll out the pastry on a lightly floured surface and use to line a 25 cm (10 inch) loose-bottomed flan tin, 4 cm (1½ inches) deep. Prick the base here and there with a fork and chill for 20 minutes.

2 Meanwhile, put the raspberries into a saucepan and sprinkle over 75 g (3 oz) of the sugar. Place over a medium heat and leave for 2 minutes, shaking the pan every now and then, until the juices have started to run from the fruit and the sugar has dissolved. Remove from the heat and leave to cool.

3 Preheat the oven to 200°C/400°F/Gas Mark 6. Line the pastry case with crumpled greaseproof paper, cover the base with a thin layer of baking beans and bake for 15 minutes. Remove the paper and beans and return to the oven for 3–4 minutes. Remove, brush the inside of the case with a little of the beaten egg and return to the oven once more for 2 minutes. Remove and lower the temperature to 180°C/350°F/Gas Mark 4.

4 For the almond sponge topping, beat the butter in a bowl, then beat in the remaining sugar a tablespoon at a time until the mixture is pale and fluffy. Beat in the egg in three lots, adding one third of the ground almonds with each addition. Sift over the flour and gently fold in with the almond extract.

5 Spread the cooled raspberries over the base of the pastry case. Drop small spoonfuls of the almond sponge mixture on top and gently spread it out to the edges of the pastry case, taking care not to let the raspberries squeeze up through the filling.

6 Bake the tart for 45–50 minutes, until the sponge is golden and springy to the touch and a skewer inserted in the centre comes out clean. Remove the tart from the tin and sprinkle lightly with caster sugar. Cut into wedges and serve warm with some double cream. This tart is best served on the day it is made.

I have to confess that as a result of a great love of greengages, I asked our pastry chef, Stuart Pate, to come up with a way of making a definitive tart that would do justice to my favourite fruit. It was the soured cream, lemon and semolina that did it, and the way he arranged the halved greengages cut-side up so they looked like circles of green atolls. Very chic.

greengage, lemon and soured cream tart

SERVES 8

1 quantity of *Sweet pastry*
(see page 201)
2 medium eggs, beaten
18 greengages
65 g (2^1/$_2$ oz) softened butter
90 g (3^1/$_2$ oz) caster sugar
A small pinch of freshly grated nutmeg
200 ml (7 fl oz) soured cream
25 g (1 oz) semolina
Finely grated zest and juice of ^{1}/$_2$ small lemon

FOR THE CRUMBLE TOPPPING:
20 g (^{3}/$_4$ oz) plain flour
15 g (^{1}/$_2$ oz) chilled butter, diced
7 g (^{1}/$_4$ oz) demerara sugar

1 Roll the pastry out thinly on a lightly floured surface and use to line a lightly greased 23 cm (9 inch) loose-bottomed flan tin, 2.5 cm (1 inch) deep. Prick the base here and there with a fork and chill for 20–30 minutes.

2 Preheat the oven to 200°C/400°F/Gas Mark 6. Line the pastry case with crumpled greaseproof paper, cover the base with a thin layer of baking beans and bake for 12–15 minutes, until the edges are biscuit coloured. Carefully remove the paper and beans and return the pastry case to the oven for 3–4 minutes. Remove, brush the inside of the case with a little of the beaten egg and return to the oven once more for 2 minutes. Remove and lower the oven temperature to 150°C/300°F/Gas Mark 2.

3 For the filling, cut the greengages in half, remove the stones and arrange them, cut-side up, over the base of the tart. Cream the butter and sugar together until pale and fluffy. Gradually beat in the remaining egg, then stir in the nutmeg, soured cream, semolina, lemon zest and juice. Pour this mixture over the greengages and bake for 25 minutes until lightly set.

4 Meanwhile, for the topping, rub the flour and butter together as you would for pastry, until the mixture resembles fine breadcrumbs. Stir in the demerara sugar. After 25 minutes, sprinkle this crumble mixture over the top of the tart and bake for another 25 minutes. By then the filling should be completely set and the crumble mix lightly golden. If it is not quite brown enough, place the tart under a medium-hot grill for 30 seconds or so, until nicely coloured. Remove and leave to cool slightly. Serve warm. This tart is best served on the day it is made.

The idea for this recipe came from a long-term food hero of mine, Joyce Molyneux, who was chef and part owner of The Carved Angel restaurant in Dartmouth. She had an amazing aptitude for English cooking, making it seem a very sophisticated but friendly cuisine. However, I suspect her food had a lot more to do with her interpretation of things than anything handed down. I love this tart, cooked for me on another endless Sunday lunch by Bill and Kate Baker, who supply many of the best wines at the restaurant. I've included a quick recipe for making apple purée too, because quinces are extremely seasonal, but they give the tart a unique and delicious, almost smoky-sweet taste.

a light apple tart with quince purée

SERVES 8

900 g (2 lb) quinces (or 500 g/1 lb 2 oz dessert apples)
750 g (1½ lb) dessert apples, such as Cox's or Braeburns
100 g (4 oz) caster sugar
500 g (1 lb 2 oz) fresh puff pastry
175 g (6 oz) apricot jam
Crème fraîche, to serve

1 Peel, quarter, core and slice the quinces and put them into a pan with 75 g (3 oz) of the sugar and 3–4 tablespoons of water. Cook gently over a low heat for about 20 minutes, until tender, then tip into a bowl and mash to a purée with a fork. Leave to cool. (If you are making this tart with just apples, cook the 500 g (1 lb 2 oz) apples as for the quinces, but then tip them into a sieve set over a bowl to collect the excess juices. Mash the apples to a smooth purée with a fork.)

2 Roll out the pastry on a lightly floured surface and cut out a 30 cm (12 inch) circle, using a plate as a template. Lift on to a lightly greased baking sheet and prick the pastry here and there with a fork, leaving a 2.5 cm (1 inch) border clear around the edge. Spread the fruit purée on top, again leaving the edge clear, and chill for at least 20 minutes.

3 Preheat the oven to 200°C/400°F/Gas Mark 6. Peel and core the apples and slice them quite thinly. Arrange the slices, slightly overlapping, in circles on top of the fruit purée and then sprinkle them heavily with the remaining sugar. Bake for 30 minutes or until the pastry is crisp and golden and the edges of the apples are lightly browned.

4 Put the apricot jam into a small pan with 1 tablespoon of water or reserved apple cooking juices, if you have them, and warm gently. Press through a sieve into a bowl and then brush generously over the apples. Serve the tart warm or cold, with some crème fraîche. This tart is best served on the day it is made.

I wanted a really smooth, deeply bitter chocolate tart for this book, so Debbie and I came up with the filling using Valrhona chocolate, the best eggs and cream. It had a velvety texture to it and was indeed pleasingly bitter, but it lacked something. I turned the dish over to our new pastry chef, Stuart Pate, and he performed the miracle – just a little marmalade spread over the blind-baked tart casing. It gives the tart a marvellous bite, without compromising the flavour of the chocolate with too much orange.

bitter chocolate and marmalade tart

SERVES 8

1 quantity of *Sweet pastry*
(see page 201)
1 small egg, beaten
200 g (7 oz) plain chocolate (with
approximately 60% cocoa solids)
250 ml (8 fl oz) double cream
2 medium egg yolks
45 g (1¾ oz) softened butter
3 tablespoons fine-cut marmalade

1 Roll the pastry out thinly on a lightly floured surface and use to line a lightly greased 23 cm (9 inch) loose-bottomed flan tin, 2.5 cm (1 inch) deep. Prick the base here and there with a fork and chill for 20–30 minutes.

2 Preheat the oven to 200°C/400°F/Gas Mark 6. Line the pastry case with crumpled greaseproof paper, cover the base with a thin layer of baking beans and bake for 12–15 minutes, until the edges are biscuit coloured. Carefully remove the paper and beans and return the pastry case to the oven for 3–4 minutes. Remove, brush the inside of the case with a little of the beaten egg and return to the oven once more for 2 minutes. Set aside and lower the oven temperature to 120°C/250°F/Gas Mark ½.

3 Break the chocolate into a bowl. Bring the cream up to simmering point in a small pan, pour it over the chocolate and stir until smooth. Mix in the beaten egg and egg yolks, then strain the mixture through a sieve into a clean bowl and mix in the softened butter.

4 Spread the marmalade in a thin layer over the base of the tart case. Pour in the chocolate mixture and bake for 15–20 minutes, until just set but still quite wobbly in the centre. It will continue to firm up as it cools. Remove from the oven and leave to cool at room temperature for 1 hour before serving. Do not refrigerate. Serve cut into thin wedges. This tart is best served on the day it is made.

I must confess to never having tried curd tart until a trip to the Yorkshire Dales and to a food festival in Layburn in May 2003. This was a weekend affair that attracted 20,000 visitors, all very enthusiastic about such great local treats as this. You can buy curd cheese from most supermarkets, but it's interesting to make your own and it gives a lighter texture.

yorkshire curd tart

SERVES 6

1.2 litres (2 pints) full-cream milk
2 tablespoons rennet
¹/₂ quantity of *Rich shortcrust pastry* (see page 201)
2 medium eggs, beaten
100 g (4 oz) butter, softened
50 g (2 oz) caster sugar
A pinch of salt
¹/₄ teaspoon ground allspice
A little freshly grated nutmeg, to taste
1 rounded tablespoon fresh white breadcrumbs
100 g (4 oz) currants

1 To make the curds, put the milk into a pan and bring it just up to blood heat – 37°C (98°F). Pour it into a bowl, stir in the rennet and set it aside somewhere cool, but not in the fridge, until set. Break up the mixture a bit and tip it into a large, muslin-lined sieve set over a bowl. Cover and leave somewhere cool to drain for 8 hours or overnight, but again, do not refrigerate.

2 The next day, roll out the pastry on a lightly floured surface and use to line a 20 cm (8 inch) loose-bottomed flan tin, 4 cm (1½ inches) deep. Prick the base here and there with a fork and chill for 20 minutes.

3 Preheat the oven to 200°C/400°F/Gas Mark 6. Line the pastry case with greaseproof paper and cover the base with a thin layer of baking beans and bake for 15 minutes. Remove the paper and beans and return the pastry to the oven for 3–4 minutes. Remove, brush the inside of the case with a little of the beaten egg and return to the oven once more for 2 minutes.

4 For the filling, tip the curds out of the muslin into the sieve and press through with a wooden spoon into a clean bowl. Cream the butter and sugar together in another bowl until pale and fluffy. Gradually beat in the curds, followed by the eggs, salt, spices and breadcrumbs. Stir in the currants.

5 Pour the mixture into the pastry case and bake for 20–30 minutes, until the filling is set and lightly golden. Leave to cool, then remove from the tin and serve, cut into thin wedges. This tart is best served on the day it is made.

Nothing impressed me more about Marco Pierre White's early cooking at Harvey's in Wandsworth, south London, than his lemon tart. I remember taking part in a Lord Mayor's banquet at the Guildhall where Marco's pastry chef, Patrick Woodside, produced a lemon tart of such opulent thickness that it was like Crocodile Dundee producing his kangaroo butchering knife when faced with a mugger in New York wielding a flick knife. Call that a lemon tart; *this* is a lemon tart. Well, we've all got better at it and mine is pretty damn macho too.

classic lemon tart

SERVES 10–12

1 quantity of *Sweet pastry* (see page 201)
6 medium eggs, beaten
3 large lemons
250 g (9 oz) caster sugar
150 ml (5 fl oz) double cream

1 Roll the pastry out thinly on a lightly floured surface and use to line a lightly greased 25 cm (10 inch) loose-bottomed flan tin, 4 cm (1½ inches) deep. Prick the base here and there with a fork and chill for 20–30 minutes.

2 Preheat the oven to 200°C/400°F/Gas Mark 6. Line the pastry case with crumpled greaseproof paper, cover the base with a thin layer of baking beans and bake for 12–15 minutes, until the edges are biscuit coloured. Carefully remove the paper and beans and return the pastry case to the oven for 3–4 minutes. Remove, brush the inside of the case with a little of the beaten egg and return to the oven once more for 2 minutes. Remove and lower the oven temperature to 120°C/250°F/Gas Mark ½.

3 For the filling, finely grate the zest from 2 of the lemons, then squeeze out enough juice from all the fruit to give you 175 ml (6 fl oz). Beat the eggs and sugar together lightly until just mixed but not frothy. Mix in the lemon juice and cream, pour through a sieve into a measuring jug and stir in the lemon zest.

4 Partly pull out the oven shelf, slide in the pastry case and then pour in the filling. Carefully slide the shelf back in and bake the tart for 40–45 minutes, until just set – the mixture should still be quite wobbly in the centre but it will continue to firm up after it comes out of the oven. Remove and leave to cool but don't refrigerate it. This tart is best served on the day it is made.

This is very similar to the lemon tart, but it's so good, I just had to include it in this book. It's the addition of the accompanying orange sorbet that makes it. I would never have thought of serving such a tart with a sorbet until Mark Raffan served it up at a dinner we were doing at Gravetye Manor, in West Sussex. It makes so much more sense than serving cream or ice-cream with an already rich dish.

seville orange tart with orange sorbet

SERVES 10–12

1 quantity of *Sweet pastry* (see page 201)
6 medium eggs, beaten
4 Seville oranges (or 2 lemons and
2 ordinary oranges)
250 g (9 oz) caster sugar
150 ml (5 fl oz) double cream

FOR THE ORANGE SORBET:
200 g (7 oz) caster sugar
120 ml (4 fl oz) water
600 ml (1 pint) Seville orange juice (or
300 ml/10 fl oz each of freshly
squeezed orange and lemon juice)

1 For the orange sorbet, put the sugar and water in a pan and bring slowly to the boil, stirring occasionally to dissolve the sugar. Remove from the heat and leave to cool. Stir in the orange juice and strain into a bowl. Churn in an ice-cream maker, then transfer to a shallow plastic container and freeze until required.

2 For the pastry case, roll the pastry out thinly on a lightly floured surface and use to line a lightly greased 25 cm (10 inch) loose-bottomed flan tin, 4 cm (1½ inches) deep. Prick the base here and there with a fork and chill for 20–30 minutes.

3 Preheat the oven to 200°C/400°F/Gas Mark 6. Line the pastry case with crumpled greaseproof paper, cover the base with a thin layer of baking beans and bake for 12–15 minutes, until the edges are biscuit coloured. Carefully remove the paper and beans and return the pastry case to the oven for 3–4 minutes. Remove, brush the inside of the case with a little of the beaten egg and return to the oven once more for 2 minutes. Remove from the oven and lower the oven temperature to 120°C/250°F/Gas Mark ½.

4 For the filling, finely grate the zest from 2 of the oranges, then squeeze out enough juice from all the fruit to give you 175 ml (6 fl oz). Beat lightly with the eggs and sugar until just mixed but not frothy. Mix in the orange juice and cream, pass the mixture through a sieve into a measuring jug and stir in the orange zest.

5 Partly pull out the oven shelf, slide in the pastry case and then pour in the filling. Carefully slide the shelf back in and bake the tart for 40–45 minutes, until the filling is just set – the mixture should still be quite wobbly in the centre but it will continue to firm up after it comes out of the oven. Remove and leave to cool but don't refrigerate it.

6 To serve, carefully remove the tart from the tin and cut it into slender wedges. Place them on dessert plates and serve with a scoop of the orange sorbet alongside. This tart is best served on the day it is made.

I'm ashamed to say that I had always considered brown-bread ice cream to be rather an unpleasant proposition until I tried it recently. I thought the brown bread would make it rather mushy. The point is, though, that because the brown bread is made into breadcrumbs and baked with sugar first, then added to the ice cream at the last minute, the final ice cream has lots of lovely crunchy bits in it.

brown-bread ice cream

SERVES 4–6

1 vanilla pod
300 ml (10 fl oz) full-cream milk
4 medium egg yolks
75 g (3 oz) caster sugar, plus
2 tablespoons
300 ml (10 fl oz) double cream
100 g (4 oz) coarse brown breadcrumbs
1 tablespoon dark rum

1 Slit the vanilla pod open lengthways and scrape out the seeds with the tip of a small, sharp knife. Put the vanilla pod, its seeds and the milk into a pan and bring to the boil. Set aside for 20 minutes to infuse.

2 Beat the egg yolks and 75 g (3 oz) of the caster sugar together in a bowl until smooth. Bring the milk back to the boil, remove the vanilla pod and whisk the milk into the egg yolks. Return the mixture to the pan and cook over a gentle heat, stirring constantly with a wooden spoon, until the mixture coats the back of the spoon. Pour into a bowl and leave to cool. Stir in the cream, then cover and chill.

3 Preheat the oven to 180°C/350°F/Gas Mark 4. Spread the breadcrumbs out on a baking tray and sprinkle with the remaining sugar. Place in the oven for 10–15 minutes, until crisp and golden. Transfer to a plate and leave to cool.

4 Churn the custard in an ice-cream maker until smooth, adding the rum and caramelised breadcrumbs towards the end of the process. Spoon into a plastic container, cover and freeze until firm.

I'm very pleased to be able to include this recipe in the book because it was one of the first puddings we ever cooked back in the seventies, the early days of the restaurant. I invented it, without apology, for reheating in a microwave. It's a typical restaurant dish; pancakes ready-made, apples stewed and custard cooked before service. The pancakes are then filled with the apple, rolled up and the custard poured over. It's such a pleasure to be using this recipe again, flavoured with Julian Temperley's lovely Somerset cider apple brandy, which has an 'I can't believe it's not Calvados' taste.

apple pancakes with apple brandy custard

SERVES 8

8 dessert apples, such as Cox's
or Braeburn's
75 g (3 oz) butter
100 g (4 oz) light soft brown sugar
1/2 teaspoon ground cinnamon
A small pinch of ground cloves

FOR THE APPLE BRANDY CUSTARD:
300 ml (10 fl oz) full-cream milk
300 ml (10 fl oz) double cream
6 medium egg yolks
50 g (2 oz) caster sugar
1 tablespoon cornflour
3–4 tablespoons apple brandy
or Calvados

FOR THE PANCAKES:
100 g (4 oz) plain flour
A small pinch of salt
1 medium egg
15 g (1/2 oz) butter, melted, plus extra
for frying
300 ml (10 fl oz) full-cream milk

1 For the custard, put the milk and cream into a small pan and bring to the boil. Meanwhile, whisk the egg yolks, sugar and cornflour together in a bowl. Whisk in the hot cream and milk, then return to the pan and cook over a low heat, stirring all the time, until the mixture lightly coats the back of the spoon. It should be just hot enough to hurt your little finger. Stir in the apple brandy and set to one side.

2 For the apple filling, preheat the oven to 150°C/300°F/Gas Mark 2. Peel and core the apples and slice them into a shallow baking dish. Melt the butter in a pan, add the sugar, cinnamon and cloves and pour this mixture over the apples. Bake for about 30 minutes, until the apples are tender.

3 For the pancakes, sift the flour and salt into a bowl. Make a dip in the centre, break in the egg and add the melted butter and milk. Gradually whisk together into a smooth batter.

4 Heat an 18 cm (7 inch) non-stick frying pan over a medium-high heat. Brush the base with a little melted butter, pour in a little of the batter and swirl it around so that it thinly coats the base of the pan. Cook for about 1 minute, until golden underneath, then flip it over and cook for a few more seconds. Slide on to a plate and repeat the process until you have 16 pancakes.

5 Spoon some of the apple mixture down the centre of each pancake and roll it up. Put 2 pancakes on to each serving plate, spoon over some of the custard and serve straight away.

The slightly sour taste of buttermilk gives these pancakes a slightly tart taste that combines very effectively with the sweet, sticky, resinous flavour of maple syrup. Don't be tempted into using maple-flavoured syrup for this. Only the real thing will do. It's expensive because it takes 40 gallons of maple-tree sap to make just one gallon of syrup.

buttermilk pancakes with maple syrup

MAKES 20

225 g (8 oz) self-raising flour
2 teaspoons baking powder
50 g (2 oz) caster sugar
175 ml (6 fl oz) buttermilk
2 medium eggs
175 ml (6 fl oz) full-cream milk
1 teaspoon vanilla extract
50 g (2 oz) *Clarified butter* (see page 201)
Maple syrup, to serve

1 Sift the flour and baking powder into a bowl and stir in the caster sugar. Make a well in the centre and add the buttermilk, eggs and most of the milk. Gradually whisk the flour into the wet ingredients, adding a little more milk if necessary to make a smooth, fairly thick batter. Stir in the vanilla extract.

2 Heat a large, non-stick frying pan over a medium heat. Brush with a little of the clarified butter and then add 3 large spoonfuls of the batter, spaced well apart. Cook for 2 minutes, until bubbles start to appear on the surface of the pancakes and they are golden brown underneath. Turn over and cook for another minute. Transfer to a plate and keep warm while you cook the remainder, brushing the pan with more butter as necessary.

3 To serve, pile the pancakes on to warmed plates and drizzle with the remaining clarified butter. Drizzle with maple syrup and eat straight away.

As with the recipe for Madeira cake (see page 188), this was inspired by a trip to the Lake District and the Lyth Valley, where damsons have been grown since time immemorial. They are not as popular as they used to be, which is a shame because they have a concentrated plum flavour and a tartness that makes them ideal for pies like this. Just one thing: it is almost impossible and very time consuming, to stone damsons before cooking, so don't. Just take care when eating.

damson cobbler

SERVES 6–8

900 g (2 lb) damsons, stalks removed
100 g (4 oz) caster sugar
Custard, double cream or crème fraîche,
to serve

FOR THE COBBLER TOPPING:
225 g (8 oz) self-raising flour
2 teaspoons baking powder
A pinch of salt
100 g (4 oz) caster sugar,
plus 1 tablespoon
75 g (3 oz) chilled butter, diced
1 medium egg
120 ml (4 fl oz) buttermilk
15 g (¹/₂ oz) flaked almonds

1 Spread the damsons over the base of a 2 litre (3½ pint) shallow ovenproof dish and sprinkle with the caster sugar. Preheat the oven to 190°C/375°F/Gas Mark 5.

2 For the cobbler topping, sift the flour, baking powder and salt into a bowl (or put them in a food processor) and add the caster sugar. Add the butter and work together with your fingertips (or by processing) until the mixture looks like fine breadcrumbs.

3 Beat together the egg and buttermilk. Add to the dry ingredients and mix together lightly to make a soft, sticky dough. Drop walnut-sized spoonfuls of the mixture over the top of the damsons, leaving a little space between each one, then sprinkle with the flaked almonds and the remaining tablespoon of sugar.

4 Bake for 30–35 minutes, until golden and bubbling, covering the cobbler loosely with a sheet of foil if it is browning a little too quickly. It is done when a skewer pushed into the centre of the topping comes away clean. Leave to cool briefly before serving with custard, double cream or crème fraîche.

I had to slip this recipe into the book at the last minute because it was so good. We filmed the cobnut harvest at Allens Farm at Plaxtol in Kent where the farmers, the Webb family, have been self-proclaimed nutters for generations. I have a secret passion for cobnuts and so, apparently, have many others, as they contact the family for mail-order boxes of them via the internet. Samantha Petter produced this dish for our lunch. I've rarely tasted a pudding that I've enjoyed so much.

cobnut meringues with damson sauce

SERVES 4

FOR THE MERINGUES:

225 g (8 oz) cobnuts in their shells, or
100 g (4 oz) shelled hazelnuts
3 large egg whites
175 g (6 oz) caster sugar
Pouring double cream, to serve

FOR THE DAMSON SAUCE:

450 g (1 lb) damsons
100 g (4 oz) caster sugar
120 ml (4 fl oz) water

1 Preheat the oven to 200°C/440°F/Gas Mark 6. Crack open the nuts, place the kernels on a baking tray and roast for 25–30 minutes until brown and crunchy – just keep checking them towards the end. Then remove, leave to cool and chop roughly.

2 Lower the oven temperature to 110°C/225°F/Gas Mark ¼. In a large bowl, whisk the egg whites to stiff peaks. Gradually whisk in the sugar to make a very stiff and shiny meringue. Stir in the chopped cobnuts.

3 Drop 8 large spoonfuls of the mixture on to a baking tray lined with baking parchment and bake for 8–10 hours, until the meringues have dried out and sound hollow when tapped underneath. Turn off the oven and leave the meringues to cool inside – this helps to stop them cracking.

4 For the damson sauce, put the damsons into a pan with the sugar and water and cook over a gentle heat for about 30 minutes, until soft. Tip the fruit into a fine sieve set over a small pan and let the syrup drain through. Add a little more sugar to the syrup, if necessary, then bring to the boil and cook until thick and syrupy. Leave to cool.

6 To serve, put two of the meringues on to 4 plates, pour around some cream and then some of the damson sauce and serve straight away.

I don't know if I'm in a minority, but I prefer my trifle without fruit. I find the combination of a good, sandy sponge lightly soaked with a really good sherry, home-made custard and some whipped cream is enough. I'm not adamant about this but if you like fruit may I suggest some thinly sliced, aromatic peaches rather than softer, more tart fruit.

traditional english trifle

SERVES 8

1/2 quantities of the ingredients for
Madeira cake on page 188, but using
2 medium eggs and omitting
the citrus peel
300 ml (10 fl oz) full-cream milk
750 ml (1 1/4 pints) double cream
6 large egg yolks
2 rounded tablespoons cornflour
4 tablespoons caster sugar
4 tablespoons good-quality
raspberry jam
6 tablespoons Oloroso (sweet) sherry

1 Preheat the oven to 180°C/350°F/Gas Mark 4. Make the cake mixture as described on page 188 and place in a greased and base-lined 450 g (1 lb) loaf tin. Level the top and bake for 30–45 minutes, until a skewer inserted in the centre comes out clean. Cool in the tin for 10 minutes, then turn out on to a wire rack and leave to cool completely. The cake can be made up to 4 days in advance and kept tightly wrapped in cling film.

2 For the custard, bring the milk and 300 ml (10 fl oz) of the cream to the boil in a non-stick saucepan. Beat the egg yolks, cornflour and sugar together in a bowl, then gradually whisk in the hot milk and cream. Return the mixture to the pan and cook over a low heat, stirring constantly, for about 10 minutes, until the mixture has thickened enough to coat the back of the spoon. Take care not to let it boil or it will curdle. Transfer the custard to a bowl and leave to cool.

3 Cut the Madeira cake into slices 1 cm (½ inch) thick and arrange a single layer over the base of the bowl. Spread the layer with 2 tablespoons of raspberry jam and lay another layer of cake on top (you might not need to use all the cake). Spread the second layer with another 2 tablespoons of raspberry jam and sprinkle over the sherry.

4 Pour the custard over the cake, cover with cling film and chill for at least 3 hours. Whip the remaining cream into soft peaks. Uncover the trifle, spoon over the cream and return it to the fridge until you are ready to serve.

I've long been looking for the perfect accompaniment to gooseberries. I love them dearly but think they don't get sympathetic treatment. I knew I'd finally got it when I made this dish and the colours worked together so well – the off-white of the rice pudding with the pale green gooseberry compote. It looked like one of those interiors magazine spreads for National Trust paint schemes. I'm a great fan of rice pudding anyway – one truly affectionate memory I have of boarding-school food – and the combination is a delight.

baked rice pudding with gooseberry compote and cream

SERVES 4

75 g (3 oz) pudding rice
50 g (2 oz) caster sugar
25 g (1 oz) butter, diced
1.2 litres (2 pints) full-cream milk
1 vanilla pod, slit open
Double cream, to serve

FOR THE GOOSEBERRY COMPOTE:
450 g (1 lb) gooseberries,
topped and tailed
225 g (8 oz) caster sugar
Pared zest and juice of 1 lemon

1 For the compote, put the gooseberries into a pan with the sugar and lemon zest and juice. Simmer for 10 minutes, until the gooseberries are tender but still holding their shape. Leave to cool and then chill for 2–3 hours.

2 For the rice pudding, preheat the oven to 150°C/300°F/Gas Mark 2. Lightly butter a 1.5 litre (2½ pint) ovenproof dish. Put the rice, sugar, butter, milk and vanilla pod into the dish and give it a good stir. Bake for 1½ hours, stirring in the skin every 30 minutes for the first hour. Then leave to bake for the last 30 minutes undisturbed, so that a golden-brown skin forms on top.

3 Remove the vanilla pod and serve the hot rice pudding with the cold gooseberry compote and some double cream.

Black rice is much used in Asia for sweet dishes and has recently swept through smart restaurants in Australia, whence this recipe came via our pastry chef from Queensland, Anita Pearce. You can buy it in this country from Asian food stores or any good deli. It has a pleasing *al dente* quality, even when long cooked. This is a great favourite of mine at the Seafood Restaurant, it's not at all filling and I'm very fond of the combination of mango and coconut.

black-rice pudding with mango sorbet and coconut milk

SERVES 6–8

300 g (11 oz) black rice
A small pinch of salt
750 ml (1¼ pints) full-cream milk
1.25 litres (2¼ pints) water
2 slices of peeled fresh ginger
225 g (8 oz) light muscovado sugar
400 ml (14 oz) can of coconut milk,
chilled, to serve

1 For the mango sorbet, make the lemon juice up to 300 ml (10 fl oz) with cold water. Put the juice, sugar and liquid glucose into a pan and bring slowly to the boil, stirring occasionally to dissolve the sugar. Remove from the heat and leave to cool.

2 Peel the mangoes and slice the flesh away from the stone. Put the flesh into a food processor and blend to a smooth purée. Stir in the lemon syrup, pass through a sieve and then churn in an ice-cream maker. Transfer to a shallow plastic container, cover and freeze until required.

FOR THE MANGO SORBET:

Juice of 2 lemons

200 g (7 oz) caster sugar

75 g (3 oz) liquid glucose

3 ripe mangoes, weighing about

450 g (1 lb) each (or 600 ml/

1 pint canned mango pulp)

3 For the black-rice pudding, put the rice into a pan with the salt, milk, water and ginger. Bring to the boil, then reduce the heat and simmer gently, stirring now and then, for 1½ hours. Add the sugar 10 minutes before the end of cooking, by which time the rice should be tender and suspended in a thick, dark purple liquid. Remove and discard the slices of ginger, transfer the rice pudding to a glass serving bowl and leave to cool.

4 Remove the mango sorbet from the freezer 10–15 minutes before you want to serve it, to allow it to soften slightly. Spoon the rice pudding into shallow serving bowls and top with a scoop of the sorbet. Pour over a little of the ice-cold coconut milk and serve straight away.

This is exactly the sort of pudding I like. No more than a full stop to an excellent meal, light and insubstantial, yet thoroughly satisfying. It makes a great deal of difference to use a good white wine for syllabub. I particularly like the spicy Gewürztraminer, with its taste faintly reminiscent of lychees, or an English wine called Bacchus made by Camel Valley Vineyard (tel: 01208 77959).

white wine syllabub

SERVES 6

**Finely grated zest and juice of
1 large lemon
2 tablespoons brandy
50 g (2 oz) caster or icing sugar
150 ml (5 fl oz) medium-dry, spicy
white wine
300 ml (10 fl oz) double cream
Sponge fingers, to serve**

Mix the lemon zest and juice, brandy, sugar and white wine together in a bowl. Cover and chill for at least an hour.

The next day, strain the wine mixture, discarding the lemon zest. Put the cream into a bowl and begin to whisk, slowly adding the wine mixture until the cream loosely holds its shape and leaves a ribbon on the surface when trailed from the whisk. Don't be tempted to whisk for too long or it will curdle.

Spoon the syllabub into tall glasses or small cups and leave somewhere cool until you are ready to serve. They can be decorated with a small twist of lemon peel, if you wish. Serve with sponge biscuits.

The food heroes for this recipe are a couple of beekeepers at Struan Apiaries, near Conon Bridge in Scotland. Hamish and Nigel Robertson produce a heather honey that has a remarkably complex flavour, like great Sauternes with – I'm not making this up – a lingering aftertaste of peat. Just for a change, this dessert is made in one large dish. I find individual restaurant portions curiously unappealing at home.

baked egg custard with caramelised honey syrup

SERVES 6

400 ml (14 fl oz) double cream
175 ml (6 fl oz) full-cream milk
5 large egg yolks
75 g (3 oz) runny honey

FOR THE CARAMELISED HONEY SYRUP:
150 g (5 oz) runny honey
3 tablespoons cold water

1 Preheat the oven to 160°C/325°F/Gas Mark 3. Put the double cream and milk into a pan and slowly bring to the boil. Meanwhile, mix the egg yolks and honey together in a large bowl.

2 Gradually beat the hot cream and milk into the yolks. Strain into a 1.5 litre (2½ pint) shallow ovenproof dish (the mixture should be about 2.5 cm/1 inch deep) and put the dish into a small roasting tin. Pour enough hot water into the tin to come half way up the sides of the dish and bake for 50 minutes, or until lightly browned on top and just set but still slightly wobbly in the centre. It will continue to firm up once it comes out of the oven. Remove the dish from the roasting tin and either leave to cool slightly to room temperature, or cover and chill for 2–3 hours.

3 For the caramelised honey syrup, put the honey into a small, heavy-based pan and leave it to boil over a high heat for a few minutes until it has caramelised and darkened slightly. Remove from the heat and add the hot water – it will splutter quite ferociously, so take care. Return the pan to a low heat and stir until smooth, then leave to go cold.

4 To serve, spoon the egg custard into bowls and pour over the caramelised honey syrup.

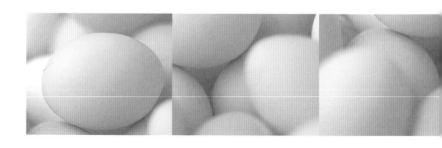

This incredibly popular pudding needs no introduction, except to say that when it's on in the restaurant it's notable how many times people comment, particularly the men, 'Oh go on then, I'll have the sticky toffee pudding.'

sticky toffee pudding

SERVES 8

175 g (6 oz) stoned dates,
coarsely chopped
300 ml (10 fl oz) water
1 teaspoon bicarbonate of soda
1 teaspoon vanilla extract
50 g (2 oz) softened butter
175 g (6 oz) caster sugar
2 medium eggs
225 g (8 oz) plain flour
1 teaspoon baking powder
150 ml (5 fl oz) clotted cream or
whipped double cream, to serve

FOR THE TOFFEE SAUCE:
300 ml (10 fl oz) double cream
225 g (8 oz) dark soft brown sugar
100 g (4 oz) butter

1 Preheat the oven to 180°C/350°F/Gas Mark 4. Put the dates, water, bicarbonate of soda and vanilla extract into a pan and bring to the boil. Remove from the heat and set aside.

2 Beat the butter and sugar together until pale and fluffy. Beat in the eggs one at a time, adding a tablespoon of the flour with the second egg if the mixture looks as if it is about to curdle. Sift the remaining flour with the baking powder and gently fold it in.

3 Bring the date mixture back to the boil. Slowly beat the liquid into the creamed mixture to make a smooth batter, then stir in the dates. Pour into a greased and lined 20 x 24–25 cm (8 x 9½–10 inch) cake tin, about 3 cm (1¼ inches) deep, and bake for 30 minutes or until a skewer inserted into the centre of the pudding comes away clean.

4 Meanwhile, put all the ingredients for the toffee sauce into a pan and leave over a low heat, stirring occasionally, until the sugar has melted. To serve, cut the pudding into 8 pieces and place on warmed serving plates. Bring the sauce back to the boil, pour it over the pudding and serve with a spoonful of cream.

This is a brilliant recipe. It comes from a hero of mine called Paul Heathcote, whose restaurants, all of which bear his name, proudly champion British food, and Lancashire cooking in particular. It's so successful because the ratio of bread to custard is exactly right. It's very important to use a fresh tin loaf and thinly cut the slices yourself, about 5 mm (¼ inch) thick. Thicker slices will absorb all the custard and make the pudding too stodgy. The custard also needs to be slightly undercooked – the French have a word for it, *baveuse.* And the crowning glory of Paul's recipe is the heavy dusting of icing sugar sprinkled on at the last minute and glazed under a hot grill until golden and crunchy.

caramelised bread and butter pudding

SERVES 6–8

6–7 thin slices of white bread, crusts removed
50 g (2 oz) butter
100 g (4 oz) sultanas
250 ml (8 fl oz) double cream
250 ml (8 fl oz) full-cream milk
3 medium eggs
50 g (2 oz) caster sugar
1 vanilla pod
25 g (1 oz) icing sugar
25 g (1 oz) apricot jam, warmed and sieved
Clotted cream, to serve

1 Preheat the oven to 190°C/375°F/Gas Mark 5. Generously spread the slices of bread with the butter and then cut each slice into 4 triangles. Arrange a layer of the bread over the base of a buttered 1.5 litre (2½ pint) shallow ovenproof dish, about 6 cm (2½ inches) deep. Sprinkle over the sultanas and then arrange the remaining bread triangles on top.

2 Mix the cream, milk, eggs and sugar together and pass through a sieve. Slit open the vanilla pod, scrape out the seeds and whisk them into the custard. Pour the custard over the bread and leave to soak for 5 minutes.

3 Put the dish into a roasting tin and pour enough hot water into the tin to come half way up the sides of the dish. Bake for about 30 minutes, until the top is golden and the custard has lightly set and is still quite soft in the centre. Remove the dish from the roasting tin and leave to cool for about 15 minutes. Meanwhile, preheat the grill to its highest setting.

4 Dust the top of the pudding heavily with the icing sugar and glaze under the grill until golden. If it starts to 'soufflé' (puff up), remove from the grill and let it cool a little longer before returning to the heat. Brush the top with the sieved apricot jam and serve with some clotted cream, if you wish.

This recipe was inspired by a heartening visit to Dalefoot farm in the village of Mallerstang, near Kirkby Stephen. Diane Halliday and her ladies were all Cumbrian farmers' wives who had had to find a way of supplementing dwindling farm incomes, made much worse by the foot and mouth crisis. They had got together and were making some really excellent cakes using the best local produce, which they then sold at all the nearby farmers' markets. This was a particular favourite of mine. For this, I find that a conventional oven is better for baking than a fan oven, which tends to dry the cake out.

madeira cake

MAKES 1 X 18 CM (7 INCH) CAKE

175 g (6 oz) butter, at room temperature
175 g (6 oz) caster sugar
3 large eggs
250 g (9 oz) self-raising flour
About 3 tablespoons full-cream milk
Finely grated zest of 1 lemon
1–2 thin pieces of candied citron or
lemon peel, to decorate

1 Preheat the oven to 180°C/350°F/Gas Mark 4. Grease an 18 cm (7 inch) round cake tin, line the base with greaseproof paper and grease the paper.

2 Cream the butter and sugar together in a bowl until pale and fluffy. Beat in the eggs, one at a time, beating the mixture well between each one and adding a tablespoon of the flour with the last egg to prevent the mixture curdling.

3 Sift over the flour and gently fold it in, with enough milk to give a mixture that falls reluctantly from the spoon. Fold in the lemon zest. Spoon the mixture into the prepared tin and lightly level the top. Bake on the middle shelf of the oven for 30 minutes.

4 Place the candied peel on top of the cake and bake for a further 30 minutes or until a warm skewer inserted into the centre comes out clean. Leave the cake to cool in the tin for 10 minutes, then turn it out on to a wire rack and leave to cool completely.

Dundee cake is my preferred fruitcake. It seems to me to have the perfect ratio of crumb to fruit and in fact I make this cake at Christmas, substituting the royal icing of the more traditional cake for the almonds. I like cities made famous by food. For me, Dundee will always be the place where the cake and the marmalade come from.

dundee cake

MAKES 1 X 20 CM (8 INCH) CAKE

100 g (4 oz) raisins
100 g (4 oz) currants
100 g (4 oz) sultanas
100 g (4 oz) glacé cherries, rinsed, dried and halved
100 g (4 oz) chopped mixed candied peel
6 tablespoons whisky
Finely grated zest and juice of ¹/₂ lemon and ¹/₂ small orange
150 g (5 oz) softened butter
150 g (5 oz) light soft brown sugar
3 large eggs, beaten
225 g (8 oz) plain flour
1 teaspoon baking powder
2–3 tablespoons full-cream milk, if necessary
25 g (1 oz) ground almonds
100 g (4 oz) blanched whole almonds, to decorate

1 Put the raisins, currants, sultanas, cherries, candied peel, 3 tablespoons of the whisky, the lemon and orange zest and juice into a bowl and stir well. Cover and leave overnight.

2 The next day, grease a 20 cm (8 inch) round, deep cake tin, line it with greaseproof paper and grease the paper. Tie a folded newspaper around the outside of the tin, then fold a second newspaper into a thick pad and place it on a baking sheet. This helps prevent the cake browning too quickly, as it is in the oven for quite a long time.

3 Preheat the oven to 160°C/325°F/Gas Mark 3. Cream the butter and sugar together until pale and fluffy. Beat in the eggs a little at a time, adding a spoonful of the flour towards the end to prevent the mixture curdling. Sift over the remaining flour and the baking powder and fold them in, adding a little milk if necessary to get a soft, dropping consistency. Fold in the ground almonds and then the soaked mixed fruit and any remaining juices.

4 Spoon the mixture into the prepared tin and level the top with the back of a spoon. Decorate the cake with circles of blanched almonds, working from the outside edge inwards and pressing them in only very lightly, or they will sink during baking.

5 Bake the cake in the centre of the oven on the newspaper-padded baking sheet for about 2 hours, until a skewer pushed into the centre comes away clean. Cool the cake in the tin for 30 minutes, then turn it out on to a wire rack and leave until completely cold. Wrap the cake in a large sheet of greaseproof paper, then in foil, and store in an airtight tin.

6 The day after baking, unwrap the cake, turn it over and prick the base with a fine skewer. Drizzle over 1 tablespoon of the remaining whisky, then re-wrap it and return it to the tin. Repeat this 'feeding' process twice more, on day 3 and day 5 after baking. Then leave the cake for a further 2–3 weeks before eating.

This recipe for white soda bread comes from Ken Buggy who, with his wife, runs the Glencairn Inn just outside Lismore in County Waterford, Eire. It is a place of such delicious Irish eccentricity; the food is wonderful and the bedrooms are like staying in the house of a sensible aunt who reads lots of jolly good books. The recipe below is pretty much how Ken gave it to us, except we have added some salt.

ken buggy's white soda bread

MAKES 1 LOAF

3 good-sized teacups of good-quality plain white flour (about 375 g/13 oz)
1 teaspoon salt
1 slightly rounded teaspoon of bread soda (bicarbonate of soda)
A tablespoon or so of cream or soured cream (optional)
300 ml (10 fl oz) buttermilk

1 Turn the oven on to 220°C/425°F/Gas Mark 7 and flour a baking tray. Sift the flour and salt into a bowl and then sift in the soda, leaving a tiny 'ball' or two in the bottom of the sieve and setting it aside, in case you get distracted and can't remember whether you've added it.

2 If you have bought a bottle or carton of buttermilk, give it a shake before opening. Before adding this to the flour, mix the flour and soda together well.

3 If you have found some cream or soured cream put it in, but if you haven't got any don't worry. It just adds a biscuit-like, crumbly texture to the bread.

4 Mix in the buttermilk – a sufficient amount to 'glue' all the flour together and to ensure that the entire mixture comes cleanly away from the sides of the bowl. If the mixture is too wet, simply add a fistful of flour. Avoid using your hands too much, as you don't want to compact the mixture. The importance is to allow plenty of air in.

5 When the mixture is a happy ball of craggy flour, you can put your hands in and, as delicately as possible, try to mould it to produce an even happier ball of flour with a smooth exterior, all the time avoiding pounding the flour like a Sicilian mamma.

6 Gently push your hands underneath the ball (imagine lifting a tiny baby from the bath) and place it on the floured tray.

7 Taking a knife, plunge it down into the doughy mixture, making a deep cross, so that your knife nearly touches the bottom, almost separating the dough into 4 pieces. You may have to smooth and repair untidy fissures with the knife, dipped in leftover buttermilk.

8 Place the tray in the middle of the oven and bake for 25–30 minutes, but don't worry if it goes to 35. Take the loaf out, turn it over and bake for another 5 minutes or so. Test the loaf by knocking it on the bottom with your knuckles. If the bread sounds hollow, then it is cooked. Leave it in a cool place for half an hour. Do not attempt to cut the bread before it is cool. This is not a great bread for keeping, but it does freeze well.

Things that might go wrong …
• Bread too yellow – too much bicarbonate of soda.
• Soggy in the middle – not long enough in the oven.
• Soggy in the middle and burnt on top – temperature too high.
• Too doughy – too much cream.
• White spots in the bread – flour too lumpy and needed to be sifted, or you didn't sift the soda.
• Bread didn't rise – forgot the soda, or the bread was left too long before putting in the oven.

The secret of good soda bread lies in the flour; it must be stoneground. For a wholemeal loaf, you need a coarsely ground flour to give the bread that incomparable crunchy nuttiness. Mount Pleasant Windmill at Kirton-in-Lindsey in Lincolnshire mills a fantastic flour especially for making this bread. The other vital ingredient is buttermilk. Supermarket buttermilk is fine but if you're lucky enough to get buttermilk that is the by-product of making butter, the flavour will be even better. Either way, it will give the bread a slight acidity, which is one of its main characteristics.

wholemeal irish soda bread

MAKES 1 LOAF

275 g (10 oz) stoneground
wholemeal flour
275 g (10 oz) plain white flour, plus a
little extra for kneading
1 rounded teaspoon bicarbonate of soda
1 teaspoon salt
450 ml (15 fl oz) buttermilk

1 Preheat the oven to 230°C/450°F/Gas Mark 8. Mix the dry ingredients together in a bowl. Make a well in the centre, pour in the buttermilk and mix together to make a soft but not too sticky dough. Add a little more buttermilk if the dough seems a bit dry.

2 Turn the mixture out on to a lightly floured surface and knead lightly and very briefly into a round. Flip the dough over and gently flatten it into a disc about 4 cm (1½ inches) thick. Lightly dust a large baking sheet with flour, place the dough on it and then, using a large knife, cut a large cross in the top, almost all the way through the dough. Stab each quarter once in the centre with the point of the knife.

3 Bake the loaf on the middle shelf of the oven for 15 minutes, then lower the oven temperature to 200°C/400°F/Gas Mark 6 and bake for a further 20–25 minutes, until it sounds hollow when you tap the base. Remove from the oven and leave to cool before serving.

accompaniments & basic recipes

accompaniments

All recipes serve 4 unless otherwise stated

plain boiled potatoes

Choose 900 g (2 lb) slightly waxy potatoes that won't break up too much in the water. I like Ratte (also known as Cornichon or Asparges), Belle de Fontenay, Charlotte, Pink Fir Apple, Jersey Royals and a red-skinned potato called Roseval. Rub or scrape off the skins, then put the potatoes into a large pan of cold water and add 1 teaspoon of salt for every 600 ml (1 pint) water. Add a good sprig of mint to the new potatoes. Bring to the boil and simmer for about 15–20 minutes, until tender – there should be no resistance when the potatoes are pierced with the tip of a knife. Drain them well, toss with a little butter if you wish, and serve straight away.

mashed potatoes

Cut 900 g (2 lb) peeled floury potatoes into chunks and put them into a pan of well-salted water (1 teaspoon salt per 600 ml/1 pint water). Bring to the boil and simmer for 15–20 minutes, until tender. Drain and leave until the steam has died down, then pass through a potato ricer or mash them. Return to the pan and fold in 50 g (2 oz) butter, some salt and white pepper to taste, and enough milk to give a smooth, creamy mash.

roast potatoes

Preheat the oven to 220°C/425°F/Gas Mark 7. Cut 900 g (2 lb) peeled floury potatoes into large chunks. Put into a pan of well-salted water (1 teaspoon salt per 600 ml/1 pint water), bring to the boil and simmer for 10 minutes, until soft on the outside but still slightly hard in the centre. Drain and leave for the steam to die down, then return the potatoes to the pan, cover with a lid and shake gently to rough up the edges a little. Heat a layer of sunflower oil, goose fat, butter or dripping in a large roasting tin, add the potatoes and turn them over once or twice until well coated in the oil. Drain off any surplus fat and roast in the top of the oven, turning the potatoes over half way through, for 1 hour, until crisp and richly golden.

chips

Peel 550 g (1¼ lb) medium-sized floury potatoes. These are the shapes I like: for thin chips, cut them into slices 8 mm (⅓ inch) thick and then lengthways into chips; for roughly cut chips, cut the potatoes into wedges; for goose-fat chips (see below), cut them into slices 1 cm (½ inch) thick and then lengthways into chips 2 cm (¾ inch) wide. Quickly rinse the chips under cold water to remove the starch and then dry them well on a clean tea-towel.

Next the oil. I like to cook most chips in groundnut oil, as it is more stable at higher temperatures, but sunflower and vegetable oil are fine, too. They are also fantastic cooked in olive oil for certain dishes – just ordinary olive oil, not extra virgin. For goose-fat chips, you will need to empty about two 340 g cans of goose fat into a medium-sized pan, so that when it has melted you have a sufficient depth in which to cook the chips – the pan should not be more than a third full. Heat the oil or goose fat to 120°C/250°F. Drop a large handful of the chips into a chip basket, lower it into the oil and cook in batches for about 5 minutes, until the chips are tender when pierced with the tip of a knife but have not taken on any colour. Lift them out and leave to drain, then chill if you don't want to cook them straight away. To finish, heat the oil or fat to 190°C/375°F and cook the chips in batches for about 2 minutes, until crisp and golden. Drain on kitchen paper then sprinkle with salt and serve straight away.

sautéed potatoes

Cut 675 g (1½ lb) peeled floury potatoes into 4 cm (1½ inch) pieces. Put them into a pan of well-salted water (1 teaspoon salt per 600 ml/1 pint water), bring to the boil and simmer until tender – about 7 minutes. Drain well and leave until the steam has died down. Heat 40 g (1½ oz) butter and 3 tablespoons olive oil in a large, heavy-based frying pan. It's important not to overcrowd the pan, so if you've not got a really large pan, use 2 smaller ones. Add the potatoes and fry them over a medium heat for about 10 minutes, turning them over as they brown, until they are crisp, golden brown and sandy – the outside of the potatoes should break off a little as you sauté them to give them a nice crumbly, crunchy crust. Season with a little salt and freshly ground black pepper and serve straight away.

sautéed potatoes lyonnaise

Cut 675 g (1½ lb) peeled floury potatoes into 4 cm (1½ inch) pieces. Put them into a pan of well-salted water (1 teaspoon salt per 600 ml/1 pint water), bring to the boil and simmer until tender. Drain well and leave until the steam has died down, then return to the pan, cover with a lid and shake gently to roughen up the edges a bit. Heat 40 g (1½ oz) goose fat or a mixture of 40 g (1½ oz) butter and 3 tablespoons sunflower oil in a large, heavy-based frying pan. Add the potatoes and fry over a medium heat for 10–15 minutes, turning them over as they brown, until they are crisp, golden brown and sandy – the outside of the potatoes should break off a little as you sauté them to give them a nice crumbly, crunchy crust. At the same time, heat another 25 g (1 oz) goose fat or butter in another pan and gently fry 1 thinly sliced large onion for about 10 minutes, until pale golden brown. Mix the onion into the potatoes and sauté together for 2 minutes, then sprinkle with a little seasoning and serve straight away.

baked potatoes

Preheat the oven to 220°C/425°F/Gas Mark 7. Scrub clean four 250–275 g (9–10 oz) baking potatoes, pierce each one on either side with the tip of a knife and sprinkle with a little salt and freshly ground black pepper. Put the potatoes directly on to the rack near the top of the oven and bake for about 1¼ hours, until tender. Remove from the oven, cut in half and squeeze gently to break open the potato. Dot each half with a knob of butter and serve.

new potatoes baked en papillote with thyme

Scrape clean 900 g (2 lb) very fresh small new potatoes. Cut out four 38 cm (15 inch) squares of greaseproof paper and foil and then put the foil squares on top of the paper ones. Divide the potatoes between the squares, sprinkle with salt and add a sprig of thyme and 25 g (1 oz) butter to each one. Bring one side of the square over the potatoes so that the edges meet. Starting at one end of the opening, fold over about 1 cm (½ inch) of the edge, doing about 4 cm (1½ inches) at a time. Work all your way around the edge to make a semi-circular parcel. Then go around again to make an even tighter seam. Finally, bash the folded edge with a rolling pin. Put the parcels on a baking sheet and bake at 220°C/425°F/Gas Mark 7 for 25 minutes. Transfer to small plates and take to the table, so that people can open up their own parcels.

quick dauphinoise potatoes

Serves 6

Slice 900 g (2 lb) peeled floury potatoes very thinly – by hand, on a mandolin or in a food processor. Put 300 ml (10 fl oz) cream, 300 ml (10 fl oz) milk, 1 crushed clove of garlic and some salt and pepper into a large non-stick saucepan and bring to a simmer. Add the potatoes and simmer for 10 minutes, turning them over gently now and then so as not to break the slices, until they are just tender when pierced with the tip of a small, sharp knife. Stir in some nutmeg and a little more salt and pepper to taste. Spoon the mixture into a lightly buttered 1.5 litre (2½ pint) shallow ovenproof dish, overlapping the top layer of potatoes neatly, if you wish. Bake in an oven preheated to 200°C/400°F/Gas Mark 6 for 30–35 minutes, until golden and bubbling.

champ

Cut 900 g (2 lb) peeled floury potatoes into chunks and put them into a pan of water salted at the rate of 1 teaspoon per 600 ml (1 pint). Bring to the boil and simmer until tender. Meanwhile, put 250 ml (8 fl oz) milk into another pan with about 225 g (8 oz) sliced fat salad onions or spring onions and simmer for 3–4 minutes, until the onions are tender. Drain the potatoes and leave until the steam has died down to make them as dry as possible. Pass them through a potato ricer, or mash, and return to the pan. Mix in the milk and onions and season to taste with salt and freshly ground white pepper. Spoon on to 4 warmed plates, shaping the mixture into mounds, and make a dip in the top. Add a 25 g (1 oz) lump of softened salted butter to each one and serve piping hot.

rösti potatoes

Boil 1 kg (2¼ lb) even-sized firm, waxy, maincrop potatoes such as Ulster Sceptre, Russet or Desiree in their skins until just tender. Drain, cool and leave overnight in the fridge. The next day, peel the potatoes and grate coarsely. Sprinkle with ½ teaspoon salt and 20 turns of the black peppermill and toss together so that they are well seasoned. Heat a heavy-based 20–23 cm (8–9 inch) frying pan over a high heat. Add 15 g (½ oz) butter and ½ tablespoon olive oil and, when the butter has melted, add the grated potatoes. Press them down lightly with a palette knife and neaten up the edges. Turn the heat down to medium and fry for 10 minutes or until crisp and richly golden underneath. Cover the pan with an inverted plate or small

as I find this gives them a less watery taste and, if you are serving them with a roast, the cooking water makes a very fresh-tasting gravy.

Allow 1 large Savoy cabbage or 550 g (1¼ lb) of the other vegetables for 4 people. Cut the cabbage into quarters, remove the core and cut each piece lengthways into slices 1 cm (½ inch) thick. Cut the stalk from the head of broccoli and break the head into smaller florets. Trim the base of sprouting broccoli and remove the first 2 or 3 leaves from each stalk. Put 1 cm (½ inch) water into a large pan, bring to the boil and add 1 teaspoon of salt and the greens. Cook over a vigorous heat, turning over now and then, for 3–4 minutes, until they are just cooked through but still slightly crisp. Drain and serve.

sautéed cabbage with smoked bacon

Cut 1 green cabbage into quarters, cut out the core, slice the pieces into strips 2 cm (¾ inch) wide and pull them apart. Heat 1 tablespoon sunflower oil in a large saucepan, add 125 g (4½ oz) cubed pancetta or streaky bacon and fry over a medium heat for 2–3 minutes, until lightly browned. Add 1 crushed small garlic clove, 15 g (½ oz) butter, the prepared cabbage, 2 tablespoons water, ½ teaspoon salt and 20 turns of the black peppermill. Cover and cook over a medium heat for 5 minutes, stirring now and then, until the cabbage has wilted down into the pan and is tender.

braised celery

Bring 600 ml (1 pint) *Chicken stock* (see page 200) to the boil and boil rapidly until reduced by half. Cut 3 celery hearts lengthways into quarters through the root. Melt 25 g (1 oz) butter in a large, shallow, heavy-based pan, add the celery and cook over a medium-high heat for 5 minutes, until very lightly coloured, turning now and then. Add the chicken stock, a scant ½ teaspoon salt and some freshly ground black pepper. Partly cover the pan and simmer for 10 minutes or until the celery is tender. Then uncover, increase the heat and boil rapidly, shaking the pan frequently, until most of the cooking juices have reduced and coated the celery in a buttery glaze. Sprinkle with a little chopped parsley.

beetroot with port and orange sauce

Peel 1 kg (2¼ lb) small beetroot and put them into a pan with 1 litre (1¾ pints) *Chicken stock* (see page 200) and 175 ml (6 fl oz) red wine. Bring to a simmer, cover and cook for about 1 hour or until tender. Lift the beetroot out of the cooking liquor and, when cool enough to handle, slice and set aside. You should be left with about 300 ml (10 fl oz) cooking liquor. If there is more, boil rapidly until reduced to the required amount. Add 85 ml (3 fl oz) ruby port, 45 g (1½ oz) redcurrant jelly and the strained juice of 1 orange and continue to boil until reduced by half. Mix 1½ teaspoons arrowroot with a little water, stir into the sauce and simmer for a further minute. Season to taste with salt and pepper. Return the beetroot slices to the sauce and simmer for a minute or two, until heated through. Transfer to a warmed dish and serve.

stir-fried bok choi with ginger, chilli and oyster sauce

Cut 675 g (1½ lb) bok choi lengthways through the root into wedges 1 cm (½ inch) thick. Heat 2 tablespoons sunflower oil in a large, deep frying pan, add 3 finely shredded garlic cloves, a finely shredded 1 cm (½ inch) piece of fresh ginger, ½ a medium-hot red chilli, seeded and thinly sliced, and

board and turn them both over together, so that the rösti is now on the plate. Return the pan to the heat with another 15 g (½ oz) butter and ½ tablespoon oil and, when it is hot, carefully slide the rösti back in. Neaten up the edges once more and cook for another 10 minutes, until golden on the other side and cooked through in the centre. Invert the rösti once more on to a board or plate and cut into quarters to serve.

potato, basil and tomato confit

Serves 4–6

Scrape 900 g (2 lb) waxy new potatoes and cut them into quarters. Heat 6 tablespoons olive oil in a pan, add 1 finely chopped onion and 2 chopped garlic cloves and cook for 5 minutes, until soft and lightly browned. Add the potatoes and 4 skinned, seeded and chopped tomatoes and cook gently for 25 minutes, until the potatoes are tender. Stir in 4 tablespoons finely shredded basil, season with salt and freshly ground black pepper and serve.

sautéed red cabbage with pears

Quarter a 675 g (1½ lb) red cabbage, remove the core and thinly slice. Melt 15 g (½ oz) butter in a large, heavy-based pan. Add the cabbage, 1 small chopped onion, 2 tablespoons light soft brown sugar, 6 tablespoons cider vinegar, a pinch each of ground cinnamon and cloves, ¼ teaspoon cayenne pepper and some salt and freshly ground black pepper. Cook over a medium-high heat, stirring now and then, for 10–12 minutes, until the cabbage is quite tender. Quarter, core and thinly slice 2 ripe but firm pears, add to the cabbage and continue to cook quite briefly until they are tender but have not broken apart. Adjust the seasoning if necessary and serve.

steamed greens

This method can be used for most greens, such as cabbage, broccoli, sprouting broccoli or Brussels sprouts. They are steamed rather than boiled,

½ teaspoon salt and stir-fry for about 15 seconds. Add the bok choi and stir-fry for about 4 minutes, until wilted and tinged with brown here and there. Add 4 tablespoons chicken stock or water, cover and cook for 2–3 minutes, until the greens are tender but still slightly crisp. Spoon over 4 tablespoons oyster sauce, shake the pan once or twice, then transfer to a warmed dish and serve.

sautéed courgettes with persillade

For the persillade, chop together 1 fat garlic clove and a handful of flat-leaf parsley leaves. Cut 450 g (1 lb) small (but not baby) courgettes into short batons. Heat 2 tablespoons olive oil in a large frying pan, add the courgettes and some seasoning and toss over a high heat for 2–3 minutes until they have taken on a little colour. Sprinkle over most of the persillade and toss together briefly. Sprinkle with the remaining persillade to serve.

deep-fried courgettes with soy sauce and panko crumbs

Cut 450 g (1 lb) courgettes on the diagonal into slices 5 mm (¼ inch) thick. Beat 2 large eggs and 2 teaspoons dark soy sauce together in a medium-sized bowl. Put 25 g (1 oz) flour and 100 g (4 oz) panko crumbs (available from Japanese shops) into 2 other bowls. Heat some oil for deep-frying to 190°C/375°F. Dip the courgette slices 6–8 at a time into the flour and knock off the excess. Dip them one at a time into the egg and then the panko crumbs and deep-fry for a minute or so, until crisp and golden. Drain briefly on kitchen paper and keep hot in a low oven while you cook the rest.

fagioli con brodo (runner beans with beef broth)

Bring 1.2 litres (2 pints) *Beef broth* (see page 200) to the boil in a pan and boil rapidly until reduced to 120 ml (4 fl oz) and very concentrated in flavour. Keep hot. Top and tail 450 g (1 lb) young runner beans and cut them lengthways into long, thin strips. Drop them into a pan of boiling well-salted water (1 teaspoon salt per 600 ml/1 pint water) and cook for 1 minute. Drain well, return to the pan with 15 g (½ oz) butter and toss together briefly. Spoon on to a serving dish, ladle over the hot beef broth and grind over a little black pepper.

french beans with tomatoes and thyme

Trim the stalk ends off 350 g (12 oz) fine green beans. Cook them in boiling well-salted water (1 teaspoon salt per 600 ml/1 pint water) for about 2 minutes, until just tender. Drain well. Put 2 tablespoons extra virgin olive oil, 2 seeded and chopped vine-ripened tomatoes, 1 chopped garlic clove, ½ teaspoon thyme leaves and some salt and pepper into the pan and place over a high heat. As soon as everything starts to sizzle, add the beans and toss together briefly. Transfer to a warmed dish and serve.

braised broad beans with dill

Gently cook 2 thinly sliced shallots in 25 g (1 oz) butter until soft but not coloured. Add 450 g (1 lb) shelled broad beans, 150 ml (5 fl oz) chicken or vegetable stock and ½ teaspoon salt. Partly cover the pan and cook gently for 4–5 minutes, until the beans are tender. Add 2 teaspoons chopped dill, cook for a few seconds longer and serve.

light green salad

This is designed to offset the richness of dishes such as Pork with cream and prunes *(page 142) or even the* Daube de boeuf Provençale *(page 116).*

Break a firm lettuce heart such as Romaine or Tom Thumb into separate leaves. Whisk together 2 tablespoons sunflower oil, 1 teaspoon white wine vinegar, 1 teaspoon Dijon mustard, ¼ teaspoon salt and a pinch of caster sugar. Toss this dressing gently through the leaves just before serving.

spring salad – escarole and gruyère cheese

Break a soft lettuce such as escarole or butterhead into separate leaves and arrange in a shallow serving dish. Sprinkle with 50 g (2 oz) tiny batons of Gruyère cheese. Whisk together 2 tablespoons olive oil, 1 teaspoon white wine vinegar, a pinch of chopped summer savory, a good pinch of salt and a little freshly ground black pepper and turn this dressing through the salad just before serving.

summer salad – italian mixed salad

A mandolin is invaluable when preparing this salad, as it slices and shreds the vegetables to the perfect size.

Serves 6
Soak a thinly sliced small red onion in a couple of changes of cold water for 10 minutes. Drain, dry on kitchen paper and put into a wide, shallow serving bowl with all the following ingredients: 2 peeled and finely shredded carrots; 1 fennel bulb, thinly cut across into horseshoe-shaped slices; ½ seeded and very thinly sliced red pepper; 1 thinly sliced celery heart; 2–3 vine-ripened tomatoes, cut into thin wedges; ½ head of curly endive, escarole or batavia lettuce, broken into bite-sized pieces; a large handful of lamb's lettuce; a small bunch of rocket. Sprinkle with ½ teaspoon salt, 2 tablespoons extra virgin olive oil and 2 teaspoons red wine vinegar. Toss together thoroughly but not roughly and serve immediately. You could substitute thinly sliced cucumber for the carrot and add finely shredded red, white or Savoy cabbage, thinly sliced radishes, and young courgette batons.

autumn salad – shaved fennel and rocket with *fines herbes* dressing

Whisk together 2 teaspoons lemon juice, 4 tablespoons extra virgin olive oil, 1 tablespoon chopped *fines herbes* (i. e. chervil, tarragon, chives and parsley) and ¼ teaspoon salt. Remove and discard the outer layer from 2 bulbs of fennel and very thinly slice the remainder lengthways through the root on a mandolin. Lay the fennel slices over a large, flat serving plate and sprinkle over a large handful of rocket leaves. Drizzle the dressing back and forth over the salad, then sprinkle with 25 g (1 oz) thinly shaved Parmesan cheese. Toss together lightly just before serving.

winter salad – savoy cabbage salad with garlic croûtons and an anchovy dressing

Remove the outer, dark green leaves from a firm Savoy cabbage. Cut it into quarters, remove and discard the core and thinly shred the remainder lengthways on a mandolin. For the croûtons, lightly toast 2 slices of white bread, cut 1 cm (½ inch) thick, then rub them on both sides with a whole peeled garlic clove. Cut the bread into cubes and fry in 20 g (¾ oz) butter until lightly golden. Drain on kitchen paper. Put 6 drained anchovy fillets into a mortar and pound with the pestle to a paste. Add 4 tablespoons extra virgin olive oil, 1½ tablespoons white wine vinegar, ½ teaspoon salt and 20 turns of the black peppermill and whisk together into a dressing. Toss the dressing with the cabbage until all the leaves are well coated, then toss in the croûtons and serve immediately.

lamb's lettuce, radicchio and green chicory salad with carpaccio dressing

Break 1 head of radicchio into bite-sized pieces, discarding the larger (and tougher) white parts of the leaves. Cut 1–2 heads of green chicory across into slices 2.5 cm (1 inch) thick. Mix the radicchio and chicory with 50 g (2 oz) lamb's lettuce and arrange over a large serving plate. For the carpaccio dressing, whisk together in a small bowl 1 medium egg yolk, 1 teaspoon white wine vinegar, ¼ teaspoon English mustard powder, ½ teaspoon salt and some freshly ground white pepper. Gradually whisk in 150 ml (5 fl oz) sunflower oil to make a mayonnaise-like mixture, then whisk in 1 tablespoon freshly squeezed lemon juice. Whisk in 2 dashes of Worcestershire sauce and 3 tablespoons milk to make a thin, pourable sauce that coats the back of a wooden spoon. Adjust the seasonings (Worcestershire sauce, lemon juice, salt and pepper) to taste, drizzle the dressing over the salad and serve.

celery heart, cos and olive salad

Hardboil 3 eggs and leave to cool. Break a Cos or romaine lettuce heart into chunky pieces and mix with 1 thinly sliced celery heart in a wide, shallow salad bowl. Whisk together 2 tablespoons olive oil, 1 teaspoon red wine vinegar and ¼ teaspoon salt and toss gently through the salad just before serving. Peel the hardboiled eggs, cut them into quarters and arrange them over the salad with 25 g (1 oz) pitted black olives and a handful of coarsely chopped flat-leaf parsley.

potato and green bean salad

Scrape 900 g (2 lb) new potatoes and cook in boiling well-salted water (1 teaspoon salt per 600 ml/1 pint water) until just tender. Drain and leave to cool, then cut lengthways into quarters and put into a salad bowl. Cook 350 g (12 oz) fine green beans in boiling salted water for 2–3 minutes, until just tender. Drain and refresh under cold water, then drain well. Add to the potatoes with some salt and pepper. Whisk together 85 ml (3 fl oz) extra virgin olive oil and 1 teaspoon red wine vinegar, add to the potatoes and beans, toss well and leave until completely cold. Just before serving, mix in 2 chopped spring onions and 2 tablespoons chopped parsley.

coleslaw

Mix together 450 g (1 lb) shredded white cabbage, 100 g (4 oz) finely chopped onion, 225 g (8 oz) coarsely grated carrot, 1 quantity of *Mayonnaise* made with mustard (see page 201), ½ teaspoon salt and some freshly ground white pepper.

steamed rice

Wash 350 g (12 oz) basmati or long grain rice in several changes of cold water until the water is relatively clear. Drain, tip into a heavy-based 20 cm (8 inch) saucepan and add ½ teaspoon salt and 600 ml (1 pint) boiling water. Quickly bring to the boil, stir once, then cover with a tight-fitting lid and reduce the heat to low. Cook basmati rice for 10 minutes and long grain for 15 minutes. Fluff up the grains with a fork and serve.

pilau rice

Heat 2 tablespoons sunflower oil in a heavy-based 20 cm (8 inch) saucepan, add 3 cloves, 3 cracked green cardamom pods, a 5 cm (2 inch) piece of cinnamon stick and a bay leaf and cook gently over a low heat for 2–3 minutes, until they become aromatic. Stir in 350 g (12 oz) of basmati rice, add 600 ml (1 pint) boiling water and ½ teaspoon salt and quickly bring to the boil. Stir once, cover with a tight-fitting lid and cook over a low heat for 10 minutes. Remove from the heat and leave undisturbed for 5 minutes, then fluff up the grains with a fork and serve.

pickled blueberries

Makes about 7–8 x 450 g (1 lb) jars

Put 600 ml (1 pint) distilled malt vinegar into a pan with 15 cloves, 6 allspice berries, a 2.5 cm (1 inch) piece of cinnamon stick, 2 small dried red chillies and 450 g (1 lb) granulated sugar. Slowly bring to the boil to dissolve the sugar, then remove from the heat and leave to stand for 2 hours. Pack 175 g (6 oz) of blueberries into 7–8 sterilised 450 g (1 lb) jars and pour over the cool syrup. Seal with vinegar-proof lids and leave for 2–3 months before using.

beetroot chutney

Makes 7 x 450 g (1 lb) jars

Peel 900 g (2 lb) raw beetroot and coarsely shred on a mandolin or by hand. Put into a preserving pan with 450 g (1 lb) chopped onions, 675 g (1½ lb) peeled, cored and roughly chopped cooking apples, 450 g (1 lb) raisins, 3 tablespoons ground ginger, 2 teaspoons dried chilli flakes, 900 g (2 lb) granulated sugar, 1.2 litres (2 pints) malt vinegar, 40 g (1½ oz) salt and the juice of 1 lemon. Heat gently, stirring, until the sugar has dissolved. Bring to the boil and simmer gently, uncovered, for about 2 hours, until well reduced and quite thick – but don't forget that it will thicken even further as it cools. Spoon into warm, sterilised jars, cover with waxed discs and then seal with vinegar-proof lids. It will keep for up to 1 year.

piccalilli

Makes about 6 x 450 g (1 lb) jars

Mix 225 g (6 oz) salt with 2.25–2.75 litres (4–5 pints) boiling water, divide between 2 large bowls and leave to cool. Prepare the vegetables: break 1 medium cauliflower into small florets, peel and halve 225 g (8 oz) pickling onions, top and tail 225 g (8 oz) runner beans and cut them into 2.5 cm (1 inch) pieces, and cut ½ large cucumber lengthways in half, scoop out the seeds and cut the cucumber into small chunks. Put the cauliflower and onions in one bowl and the runner beans and cucumber in the other. Put plates on top to submerge the vegetables and leave for 24 hours. Drain the vegetables and rinse them well, keeping them separate. Put 100 g (4 oz) caster sugar, 1 crushed garlic clove and 900 ml

sterilised jars and leave to cool. Cover with wax discs and then seal with lids. This will keep for up to 2 years, unopened.

margaret fisher's elderberry jelly

Pull the elderberries off their stems with a fork into a large, non-reactive saucepan and mix with an equal weight of chopped bramley apples (no need to peel or core). Barely cover the fruit with cold water, bring to a simmer and cook until soft and pulpy. Tip the mixture into a sterilised jelly bag suspended over a large bowl and leave the juice to drip through. Don't be tempted to squeeze the bag or the finished jelly will be cloudy. Measure the juice, pour into a pan and add 450 g (1 lb) sugar for every 600 ml (1 pint) juice. Heat gently until the sugar has dissolved, then boil rapidly until it reaches setting point (see *Minted apple and cider jelly*, left). Pot, seal and store for up to 1 year.

(1½ pints) distilled malt vinegar into a large stainless-steel saucepan. Bring to the boil, add the cauliflower, onions, ¼ teaspoon each of ground allspice and freshly grated nutmeg and cook for 3 minutes. Add the runner beans and cucumber and cook for a further 4–5 minutes. The vegetables should be only just cooked, with a little crunch left in them. Lift them out of the vinegar with a slotted spoon and place in a large bowl. Mix 25 g (1 oz) plain flour, 15 g (½ oz) each of English mustard powder and turmeric powder and 7 g (¼ oz) ground ginger with another 2½ tablespoons distilled malt vinegar and enough water to make a smooth paste. Add a little of the hot vinegar mixture to the paste, stir back into the pan and bring to the boil, stirring. Simmer for 5 minutes. Stir the sauce into the vegetables, spoon into warm, sterilised jars, seal with vinegar-proof lids and leave to cool. The pickle is ready to eat immediately and will keep for up to 1 year.

minted apple and cider jelly

Makes 8–10 x 450 g (1 lb) jars

Tie 10 sprigs of mint and the pared zest of 1 large lemon into a bunch and put in a large pan with 1.75 kg (4 lb) roughly chopped unpeeled Bramley apples and 2.25 litres (4 pints) dry cider. Bring to the boil and simmer for 25 minutes, stirring now and then, until pulpy. Pour the mixture into a sterilised jelly bag and leave it to drip over a large bowl until it stops. Don't be tempted to squeeze the bag because this will make the jelly cloudy. Return the pulp in the bag to the pan, add 1.2 litres (2 pints) water and simmer for 20 minutes. Drain through a jelly bag as before. Combine the 2 juices and measure the volume. Weigh out the granulated sugar, allowing 450 g (1 lb) for every 600 ml (1 pint) juice and set aside. Pour the apple juice into a clean pan and add the juice of 2 lemons. Bring to the boil and boil for 10 minutes. Add the sugar and stir until it has dissolved, then bring back to the boil, skimming off any scum as it rises to the surface. This is important for a really clear jelly. Boil rapidly for about 10 minutes, until setting point is reached. Test this by pouring a little jelly on to a chilled saucer. Chill for a few minutes, then push your finger across the surface. If it wrinkles, then it's ready. Take the pan off the heat and leave to cool for 10 minutes. Stir in 20 g (¾ oz) finely chopped mint, pour into warm,

OTHER SALADS AND SIDE DISHES:

Colcannon and devilled tomatoes (see page 131)
Thyme boulangère potatoes (see page 65)
Olive potato cakes (see page 135)
Hot beetroot and horseradish (see page 151)
Traditional English salad with creamy tarragon dressing (see page 98)
Fresh Russian salad (see page 86)
Lamb's lettuce, frisée and beetroot salad (see page 114)
Matchstick potatoes (see page 115)
Risotto Milanese (see page 129)
Kohlrabi and carrot salad (see page 136)
Grilled Parmesan polenta (see page 152)
Potato, bacon and truffle oil pithiviers (see page 155)
Tomato and hot red pepper salad (see page 156–7)
Tomato, roasted red pepper and black olive salad (see page 54)
Rocket salad with a soy and sesame dressing (see page 55)

basic recipes

STOCKS

All the stocks below will be much intensified if the strained stock is then simmered with 225–450 g (8 oz–1 lb) fish or chicken fillet, in the case of fish or chicken stock respectively, or shin of beef with beef stock. I quite often combine chicken stock with fish stock for stronger-flavoured fish sauces.

fish stock (fumet)
Makes about 1.2 litres (2 pints)

1 kg (2¼ lb) flat-fish bones, such as lemon sole, brill and plaice
2.25 litres (4 pints) water
1 onion, chopped
1 fennel bulb, chopped
100 g (4 oz) celery, sliced
100 g (4 oz) carrot, chopped
25 g (1 oz) button mushrooms, sliced
1 sprig of thyme

Put the fish bones and water into a large pan, bring just to the boil and simmer very gently for 20 minutes. Strain through a sieve into a clean pan, add the vegetables and thyme and bring back to the boil. Simmer for 35 minutes or until reduced to about 1.2 litres (2 pints). Strain once more and use as required. If not using immediately, leave to cool, then chill and refrigerate or freeze for later use.

chicken stock
Makes about 1.75 litres (3 pints)

Bones from a 1.5 kg (3 lb) uncooked chicken, or 450 g (1 lb)
    chicken wings or drumsticks
1 large carrot, chopped
2 celery stalks, sliced
2 leeks, sliced
2 bay leaves
2 sprigs of thyme
2.25 litres (4 pints) water

Put all the ingredients into a large pan and bring just to the boil, skimming off any scum from the surface as it appears. Leave to simmer very gently for 2 hours – it is important not to let it boil, as this will force the fat from even the leanest chicken and make the stock cloudy. Strain the stock through a sieve and use as required. If not using immediately, leave to cool, then chill and refrigerate or freeze for later use.

roasted chicken stock
Makes about 2.25 litres (4 pints)

450 g (1 lb) chicken wings or drumsticks
2 tablespoons sunflower oil
1 large carrot, chopped
2 celery stalks, sliced
2 leeks, sliced
2 bay leaves
2 sprigs of thyme
2.25 litres (4 pints) water

Preheat the oven to 200°C/400°F/Gas Mark 6. Put the chicken wings or drumsticks into a roasting tin and roast for 45 minutes or until crisp and richly golden. Meanwhile, heat the oil in a large pan, add the carrot, celery and leeks and fry until lightly browned. Transfer the roasted chicken pieces to the pan and add the herbs. Add a little of the water to the roasting tin and place it over a medium heat on top of the stove. Bring to a simmer, scraping all the caramelised juices from the base of the tin with a wooden spoon, then add to the pan with the rest of the water. Cover and leave to simmer very gently for 1 hour. Strain the stock through a fine sieve and use as required. If not using immediately, leave to cool, then chill and refrigerate or freeze for later use.

beef broth
Makes about 2.5 litres (4½ pints)

900 g (2 lb) shin of beef
2 celery stalks
2 carrots
2 onions
50 g (2 oz) piece of Parmesan rind (optional)
5 litres (8 pints) water
2 bay leaves
2 thyme sprigs
1 tablespoon salt

Put all the ingredients except the herbs and salt into a large saucepan and bring to the boil, skimming off any scum as it rises to the surface. Reduce the heat and leave to simmer for 2½ hours, adding the salt and herbs 15 minutes before the end.

duck confit
Put 50 g (2 oz) salt, 1 tablespoon thyme leaves, the leaves from 1 large sprig of rosemary, 2 thinly shredded fresh bay leaves and 2 roughly chopped garlic cloves into a spice grinder and grind together until the mixture looks like wet sand. Sprinkle half this cure over the base of a shallow dish, put 4 large duck legs on top and then cover with the rest of the cure. Cover and leave in the fridge for 6 hours, turning the legs over half way through. Don't leave any longer or the duck will become too salty. Rinse the salt cure off the duck legs and pat them dry with kitchen paper. Bring 900 g (2 lb) duck or goose fat to a gentle simmer in a large casserole, add the duck legs, making sure that they are completely submerged, then cover and transfer to an oven preheated to 140°C/275°F/Gas Mark 1. Cook for

1½ hours, then remove from the oven, leave to cool and chill until needed. To use, lift the duck legs out of the fat and wipe off as much fat as you can with kitchen paper. Use the confit legs as required in your recipe or, to serve them as a dish in their own right, remove them from the fat and wipe off most, but not quite all of it. Put them on a baking tray, skin-side up, and roast in an oven preheated to 200°C/400°F/Gas Mark 6 for 15–20 minutes, until the skin is crisp and golden and the meat has heated through.

mayonnaise

This recipe includes instructions for making mayonnaise in a liquidiser or by hand. It is lighter when made mechanically, because the process uses a whole egg, whereas hand-made mayonnaise is softer and richer. You can use sunflower oil or olive oil, or a mixture of the two if you prefer. It will keep in the fridge for up to 1 week.

Makes 300 ml (10 fl oz)

2 egg yolks or 1 egg
2 teaspoons white wine vinegar
1/2 teaspoon salt
1 tablespoon mustard (optional)
300 ml (10 fl oz) sunflower oil or olive oil

To make the mayonnaise by hand:
Make sure all the ingredients are at room temperature before you start. Put the egg yolks, vinegar, salt and mustard, if using, into a mixing bowl and then place the bowl on a cloth to stop it slipping. Using a wire whisk, lightly whisk to break the yolks, then beat the oil into the egg mixture a few drops at a time, until you have incorporated it all. Once you have added the same volume of oil as the original mixture of egg yolks and vinegar, you can add the remainder a little more quickly.

To make the mayonnaise in a machine:
Put the whole egg, vinegar, salt and mustard, if using, into a liquidiser or food processor. Turn on the machine and then slowly add the oil through the hole in the lid until you have a thick emulsion.

clarified butter

Place the butter in a small pan and leave it over a very low heat until it has melted. Then skim off any scum from the surface and pour off the clear (clarified) butter into a bowl, leaving behind the milky-white solids that will have settled on the bottom of the pan.

beurre manié

Blend equal quantities of softened butter and plain flour together into a smooth paste. Cover and keep in the fridge until needed. It will keep for the same period of time as butter.

roasted red pepper

Spear the stalk end of the pepper on a fork and turn the pepper in the flame of a gas burner or blowtorch until the skin has blistered and blackened. Alternatively, roast the pepper in an oven preheated to 220°C/425°F/Gas Mark 7 for 20 minutes, turning once, until the skin is black. Remove the pepper from the oven and leave to cool. Then break it in half and remove the stalk, skin and seeds. The flesh is now ready to use.

basic shortcrust pastry

225 g (8 oz) plain flour
1/2 teaspoon salt
50 g (2 oz) chilled butter, cut into pieces
50 g (2 oz) chilled lard, cut into pieces
11/2–2 tablespoons cold water

rich shortcrust pastry

25 g (8 oz) plain flour
1/2 teaspoon salt
65 g (21/2 oz) chilled butter, cut into pieces
65 g (21/2 oz) chilled lard, cut into pieces
11/2–2 tablespoons cold water

For either pastry, sift the flour and salt into a food processor or a mixing bowl. Add the pieces of chilled butter and lard and work together, either in the food processor or with your fingertips, until the mixture looks like fine breadcrumbs. Stir in the water with a round-bladed knife (or process briefly) until it comes together into a ball, then turn out on to a lightly floured work surface and knead briefly until smooth. Use as required.

sweet pastry

175 g (6 oz) plain flour
A small pinch of salt
50 g (2 oz) icing sugar
100 g (4 oz) chilled butter, cut into pieces
1 egg yolk
1–11/2 teaspoons cold water

For the pastry case, sift the flour, salt and icing sugar into a food processor or bowl, add the pieces of chilled butter and work together briefly, either in the food processor or with your fingertips, until the mixture looks like fine breadcrumbs. Stir in the egg yolk and enough water until the mixture starts to come together into a ball (or add to the processor and process briefly), then turn out on to a lightly floured surface and knead briefly until smooth. Use as required.

index
Page numbers in *italic* refer to the illustrations

acknowledgements

I am indebted to Debbie Major who helped test and write up the recipes for this book. As well as producing the food for the photography, she prepared the food for the TV series that it accompanies. As I said of her in my last two books, *Seafood* and *Food Heroes*, without her this book would have been years in the making.

Though my name appears on the front cover, this sort of book is very much a team effort. Much of the enjoyment of creating something like this lies in working with a group of talented people who are also friends. So, once again, I must thank James Murphy for the wonderful food photography, Craig Easton for the landscape photography, Paul Welti for the beautiful design work, Art Directors Pene Parker and Sarah Ponder, Commissioning Editor Viv Bowler and Project Editor Rachel Copus.

I would also like to thank Paul Bridgeman at Chomette for supplying us with Pillivuyt china

for use during filming and photography, David West for helping with our butchery questions, Matthew Stevens for providing us with outstanding fish to use during recipe testing, food photography and filming, Chris McCabe for his outstanding knowledge on game and butchery, and Dodie Miller at the Cool Chile Company for supplying us with unusual Mexican ingredients at a moment's notice.

Finally, thanks are due to the following for help with photography (illustrations are indicated in brackets): Doddington Dairy, Wooler, Northumberland (pages 2–3, 12–13); The Chicken Came First, Newport, Shropshire (page 4); Jekka's Herb Farm, Alveston, Bristol (pages 5, 27, 28–9); Raymond Reece and David Rees (pages 48–9); Peele's, Thuxton, Norwich (pages 91, 92–3); Farmer Sharp, Dalton-in-Furness, Cumbria (pages 110–11); Long Crichel Bakery, Wimborne, Dorset (pages 162–3).

Extract on page 74 from 'Moules à la Marinière' from *The Rule of Three* by Elizabeth Garrett (Bloodaxe Books, 1991), by kind permission of Bloodaxe Books.

bibliography

Davidson, Alan, *The Oxford Companion to Food* (Oxford University Press, 1999)
Fort, Matthew, *Paul Heathcote's Rhubarb and Black Pudding* (Fourth Estate, 1998)
Olney, Richard, *Lulu's Provençal Table* (Ten Speed Press, 2002)
Pomiane, Edouard de, *Cooking with Pomiane* (Serif, 1993)
Vence, Céline (Ed.) *Cuisine du Terroir* (Corgi Books, 1988)
Waters, Alice, *Chez Panisse Menu Cookbook* (Random House, 1982)